𝒥ₒ

PA

MW01256723

Thank you for
all your inspiration

Best regards,

Donald N. Yates

Nov. 2, 2013

Granny Dollar

Ancestors and Enemies

PHYLLIS E. STARNES and
DONALD N. YATES

Panther's Lodge

PHOENIX

ISBN: 0615906893
ISBN-13: 978-0615906898

CONTENTS

ILLUSTRATIONS

CREDITS

frontispiece The Bear Went over the Mountain, p. 223, from Alton Beason's barbershop wall, Fort Payne, Alabama. ii unidentified granddaughter of Richard Blevins. viii Eliyah Skeans from Brian Hall. 16 church for sale in Oliver, Georgia. 16 nineteenth-century songbook. 50 melungeons.com. 66 Julia Starnes. 74 George Caitlin. 98 John Wesley Monroe Dolphus Cooper, his wife Dovey Palestine and their baby, Bessie Louise, 1918. 106 Harmon Cooper tombstone, New Hope Cemetery. 116 from Chief Justice.

Blevins Cousin

YOU MIGHT BE MELUNGEON IF

Your grandfather is buried under a tombstone with a Star of David.

Someone in your family married a Portuguese.

You have a knoblike bump at the base of your brain.

You were born with six fingers on each hand.

All your ancestors came from Tennessee or Kentucky.

Your grandmother was called Mahala Jane.

There are six women named Alzina Louisa in your family tree.

You have an uncle named Milton or Furby.

You are related to Pocahontas and Christopher Columbus.

You make deals only with relatives.

You suffer from something the old folks call Indian Fever.

Your ancestors lived on property straddling two or more states or counties and were sometimes counted on the census in one place, sometimes in another place, without moving.

One line in your family claimed

simultaneously to be Scotch-Irish, German, Dutch, Portuguese, Spanish, French and English.

You marry your double cousin.

You marry your brother's widow.

Someone in your family married their niece or step-daughter, forever stumping genealogists.

Your family tree looks more like a telephone pole.

Family history is never mentioned or discussed.

You have an aunt who is Jewish and no one knows why.

Your mother has a letter at the Baptist Church, your father at the Methodist Church, they sent your brother to the Pentecostals and they sent you to the Presbyterian Church.

Your mother waves a chicken over her head once a year.

Your family goes down to the river and lets their old clothes wash away downstream every fall.

Your family makes fun of Catholics even though they have never met any.

You do not eat pork.

You eat pork.

ANCESTORS AND ENEMIES

Your father occasionally curses the King of
Spain.

Everyone in your family has one name for
outsiders and another for use within the family.
The latter are names like Linny, Creecy, Moe and
Rube.

You got married at home and the neighbors
took pot shots at the arriving wedding guests.

Most of your family were buried at home. . .
within twenty-four hours of dying.

The log cabin your pioneer forbears built has
Moorish arches.

Your great-great-great-grandparents avoided
the Trail of Tears but for unknown reasons ended
up in Oklahoma later anyway.

Your ancestors claimed they were Black Dutch.

Your ancestors denied they were Black Dutch.

Your grandparents speak of Daniel Boone and
Andrew Jackson as though they lived yesterday.

Your grandfather never set foot in church until
he died and they took him there in a coffin.

You light candles on Friday night.

You throw a dime into a baby boy's first
bathwater.

You cover all the mirrors in the house when

someone dies.

Your grandmother is called a Daughter of Israel on her tombstone.

You throw out eggs with blood spots.

Your mother has a menorah passed down to her.

You only read the Old Testament part of the Bible.

You make fun of the Blessed Virgin Mary.

You refer to Jesus as Jesus, not as Jesus Christ.

The family gathers on Christmas Eve to make toilet paper for the ensuing year.

Beggars are periodically invited to your table.

You believe in fairies showing up to name infants.

Everybody at family reunions faces east and shakes their fists at the Pope.

You clean the house on Friday and put on clean clothes on Saturday.

All the males in your family are circumcised.

You rend your clothes and overturn furniture when a relative dies.

You sweep the floor away from the door into

the center of the room, never out across the threshold.

You know which way Jerusalem lies.

You were told by your father that you were a Jew when you turned 13 (girls by their mother when they turned 12).

There is a lot of talk about Egypt and the Pharaoh in your family.

Your grandmother was a Campbellite and called her church a temple and they just read the Old Testament.

Your doctors tell you that you have some kind of arthritis but all tests come out negative and they shake their heads.

You had an aunt that sang in Hebrew at "church."

You had a grandmother and an aunt whose idea of a fashion statement was akin to Muslim dress.

Your mother shooed away Xmas carolers with no explanation.

No one ever discussed the baby Jesus at Xmas or had a manger scene and you sang only modern tunes like "Rockin' Around the Xmas Tree" and it was never written any other way than as 'Xmas.'

Xmas was just about giving gifts to family and

the poor and you got gold candy coins in your stocking.

Your mother's idea of decorating a Xmas tree was to cover it with red birds and popcorn and Xmas paper was from the Sunday funny papers or just silver or solid colors.

You heard more about Moses and Noah than you did Jesus.

You were told that you were named after someone that was Jewish though you did not know a soul that was.

It would have been worse to mention the Pope in your household growing up than to mention The Rolling Stones.

You and your cousins called your grandmother "Mammy."

Your southern granddads found it prudent *not* to enlist as Rebel soldiers— instead they retreated deep into the mountains and waited until the Civil War was over.

Your children are born with odd-looking dark spots and your Asian doctor gives you a funny look when you tell her both you and your husband are Caucasian.

Your Native American neighbor sits you down and gently explains to you that you are a mixed-race person.

ANCESTORS AND ENEMIES

While at church, an evangelical prophet point
to you and addresses you as a "Mother of Israel."

There's no world cuisine you won't eat.

You feel uncomfortable living in an all-white
community — even though you are "white."

In college, your Jewish boyfriend asks, "Are
you *sure* you're not Jewish?"

Your family seemed ethnic but no one was
copping to what kind.

*Thanks to Melungeons.com, Teresa Panther-Yates
and Kari Carpenter.*

He claimed to have both Jewish and Scottish ancestry

1 STRANGE GENES IN APPALACHIA

Albert Einstein was at a dinner party in Princeton when he held a position in physics at the Institute for Advanced Studies. The conversation turned to Einstein's recent comment that God did not play at dice. The universe was not the result of random chance entirely. Was God then evil since so many events in our lives tended to turn out badly? "The good Lord is not mean," Einstein explained, "but he's crafty."

Something similar can be said about DNA. It does not lie, but it is often rather oblique. Even geneticists—the scientists dedicated to unraveling its mysteries—are only at the beginning of understanding how it can make us smarter, taller, more artistic, better at math, prone to certain diseases, or able to excel at running long or short distances. The six-billion-marker map of our genes from the Human Genome Project was completed just a few years ago. It is still a matter of dispute exactly what a gene is in the first place. How can the layman fathom the intricacies and ever-changing revelations in such a field? It is like trying to know the mind of God.

As with most people, I possessed a very imprecise knowledge of genes and genetics, to say the least. I had only a begrudging interest in genealogy, which I considered was for the birds. Out of the blue, I got an email from Elizabeth Hirschman, a professor at Rutgers University in New Brunswick, just down the road from Einstein's august old haunts. I'll never forget the subject line: "Cooper Ethnicity?" As it turned out, Beth was a distant cousin. Like me, she was descended from a Kentucky pioneer named Isaac Cooper, whose grandfather William Cooper acted as guide and scout for Daniel Boone, and whose descendants intermarried with the Choctaw and Cherokee Indians. Was I aware that those pioneer Coopers were Melungeons, part of a rare Appalachian ethnic group? Did I know where the Coopers came from? Was I ever told they were Jewish? Did I have a male Cooper uncle or cousin of my mother, Bessie Cooper, whom she could test with DNA to confirm it?

I knew at once it was true. There was no question in my mind. It hit me like a thunderbolt. In a heartbeat, a new identity swept through my whole being. Despite the saying that nature does not like sudden leaps, I took in one breath as a Scots-Irish-part-Cherokee Southern Baptist and exhaled as a Jew.

It was time for me to lock my office door and

go home. Teresa was waiting in the parking lot. I threw my briefcase and a pile of library books in the back seat of our Camry.

"Guess what, Babe," I said. "We're Jewish . . . at least, I am."

I filled her in on Cousin Beth's email and the Melungeons. My wife and I are also cousins, so I assumed in my heady shock of recognition that her family must be Jewish as well. I didn't stop to wonder what the effect and impact of the news might be for her. A passage from a diary she kept during these times illustrates how one man's mead can be another man's poison:

I wanted to go back to before I had got in the car, before I had left our Low Country home in the pinelands. If I could just retrace my steps backwards to that safe haven of innocence! He had to be wrong. He must be wrong. Either that or I have to discover a way to make this unimportant.

"Melungeons are Sephardic Jews! My people are Jewish! We are Jewish! Your Rameys, my Coopers, most of the other lines!"

This was too, too much. Now in my forties I find I am Jewish? I thought, "I can ignore this," and I did.

The Melungeons are what anthropologists have termed a tri-racial isolate and what the ordinary person today might call people of color. They form a remote, intricately inbred population separated by history and geography from their neighbors. Their genetic background is mixed, exactly how mixed varies on a case-by-case basis. Their largest concentration lies in the rural, mountainous intersection of eastern Tennessee, western North Carolina, eastern Kentucky, western

Virginia, and southern West Virginia. Other Melungeon communities are found in southern Ohio (Mt. Carmel Indians), central Tennessee near Chattanooga (Graysville Melungeons) and Sand Mountain, Alabama (where my mother's family was from). Estimates of the size of the Melungeon population range from 50,000 to more than 250,000. They constitute a not-insignificant ingredient in the national melting pot and may qualify as America's oldest ethnic minority.

Typical surnames have been identified (Cooper among them), and characteristic medical conditions noticed, for instance, familial Mediterranean fever, an inflammatory disorder passed down in families coming originally from countries around the Mediterranean Sea. The word Melungeon could be French ("mixture"), Turkish ("accursed souls"), the name of an Angolan tribe Malunjin, or malungu, a Portuguese-African term meaning "shipmate." Theories abound. By all accounts, these enigmatic people were discovered already in place when the first English settlers crossed the Blue Ridge Mountains into the interior of North America. John Sevier, later governor of Tennessee, was one of the first to venture into Indian Country, along with the pioneer Daniel Boone, longhunters like Elisha Walden and Daniel Blevins, and Indian traders like James Adair, who wrote *History of the American Indians*. Sevier described a mysterious white mountain-dwelling people with guns, a community bell and all the marks of civilization. They spoke an unfamiliar tongue and were unusually suspicious of strangers.

Were they remnants of a Portuguese colony?

Shipwrecked Moors? Phoenicians? Welshmen? Some sort of "white Indian" tribe? Runaway slaves? Whoever they were, and wherever they came from, it was clear they did not enjoy a very savory reputation. The first recorded use of the word "Melungeon" occurs in the minutes of the Stony Creek Primitive Baptist Church in Scott County, Virginia, in 1813. One of the members, Sister Kitchen, accused another woman of harboring "them Melungins." Nashville journalist Will Allen Dromgoole, a descendant of Scottish Indian trader Alexander Dromgoole and Cherokee chief Doublehead's daughter Nanny the Pain, catapulted the Melungeons into public awareness with a series of newspaper articles in the 1890s. She painted a pretty lurid picture of them:

Their complexion is a reddish-brown, totally unlike the Mulatto . . . . They are not at all like the Tennessee mountaineer, either in appearance or characteristics . . . . The Malungeons are filthy, their home is filthy. They are rogues, natural "born rogues," close, suspicious, inhospitable, untruthful, cowardly, and, to use their own word, "sneaky." In many things they resemble the negro. They are exceedingly immoral, yet are great shouters and advocates of religion.

Insult turned to injury with Walter A. Plecker, director of Virginia's department of vital and health statistics. Appointing himself keeper of the Old Dominion's racial purity policies, and practicing a sort of paper genocide, Plecker treated Melungeons as mixed bloods trying to pass illegally as white. He kept lists of surnames (including Cooper) and registered those bearing these surnames as "mongrels." The state accordingly denied many of these people the right to vote or attend school. Melungeon families ended up going under cover, some destroying their birth certificates to conceal their origins. They tended to stop telling their children the truth of who they were. When my mother entered Berry College in Georgia, her father Dolph Cooper of Sand Mountain, Alabama, swore an affidavit that she had no birth certificate. Plecker's reign of terror lasted thirty years, from 1912 to 1942.

At this point, many readers are probably wondering why if these people were so despised and persecuted would anybody want to own up to being one of them. Remarkably, there are thousands today who cherish the idea. Popular and scientific interest in the Melungeons was revived in 1994 with the publication of *Melungeons: The Resurrection of a Proud People* by N. Brent Kennedy. Born in the Melungeon heartland in Wise, Virginia, with an extra digit on his hands (a rare genetic trait known elsewhere in the Appalachians, also in regions of Turkey), as a young man he went on to recover from a near-fatal attack of familial Mediterranean fever. Brent began investigating his own ancestry in order to discover how "a Scotch-Irish white boy could get a Mediterranean-Jewish-Arab disease," especially one requiring the presence of a recessive gene on both his mother's and father's side. Kennedy's decidedly "non-white boy" appearance, as well as those of his parents, cousins and some of the neighbors, together with his discovery of falsified family records claiming "white" ancestry, led him to speculate that he was, in fact, of Melungeon descent. His heartfelt history sparked awakenings by others. A whole new generation who had gone to bed white woke up to find themselves brown, according to Elizabeth Hirschman. "And what was (possibly) more troubling," she writes, "having gone to bed Christian, they awoke to find themselves having potentially Jewish or Muslim ancestry along with hereditary Jewish and Muslim diseases. . . . The seemingly quaint practices of their grandparents — for instance naming children Mecca, Omar, Menorah and Alzina, discarding eggs with blood spots, avoiding pork and thoroughly washing and salting all other meats — took on an ominous new meaning."

The first attempt to define Melungeons with the contemporary tools of genetics was a study by English biologist Kevin Jones, working with the University of Virginia's College at Wise and University College in London in 2000. Sampling men and women regarded as part of a "core group" from Newmans Ridge in Hancock County, Tennessee, the Jones survey found that Melungeons, on the face of it, and on average, were about 90% European, 5% Native American and 5% African — not much different from the surrounding population. This was not the whole story, though. Within the European lines of descent, "there is significant diversity, and some seem to reflect areas outside the traditional northern European sphere," noted Jones. And according to the president of the Melungeon Heritage Association, "The presence of Turkish and northern Indian haplotypes [descents] within the mitochondrial [female] DNA samples taken from modern-day Melungeons indicates that women of European/Asian origin were a part of the original mixture that made up the Melungeon ancestry." One of the female lineages in Brent Kennedy's family, for instance, proved to be of the N haplogroup (branch), the first out-of-Africa human beings. This finding put to rest the assumption that European males, marooned Spanish and Portuguese sailors perhaps, took wives with Native Americans and African-Americans to produce the Melungeons. Since mitochondrial DNA is passed exclusively by mothers to their children, and only their daughters can continue to propagate the exact type, its presence meant that women formed part of the original nucleus of the colony or settlement. The conclusion was that the Melungeons were a coherent, endogamous population group, not just an ad hoc mix that happened to bubble up on the Tennessee frontier. They had a homeland—but where?

Some players in the still-unfolding drama, a number of whom might themselves be entitled to call themselves Melungeons, rejected the very concept of Melungeons, maintaining Melungeons are one and the same with the predominantly Scots-Irish and English settlers of the surrounding region. Leading the charge for the non-believers was Virginia E. DeMarce, who released a scathing review of Kennedy's book in 1996. DeMarce assembled details from courthouse and other public records showing that the Goins, Gibson, Collins, Chavis, Riddle, Bunch and other surnames identified as Melungeon were actually surnames borne by mulattos, taxed Indians or just plain white persons moving to the frontier from the coastal settlements in Virginia and North Carolina. It remained for others to point out that the names had nonetheless an exotic element. Chavis, for instance, plainly came from the common Sephardic Jewish surname Chavez, derived from the name of a town in Portugal. Casteel probably originated with a native of Castile in Spain. Dula was the name of a Berber clan. Mozingo and Cumbow (Gumbo) were transparently African, and perhaps Muslim. Hyatt and Elliott were Arabic, as was Mustain. Tolliver came from the Spanish word for blacksmith. Lopes was Portuguese for Spanish Lopez. Hendrix was Henriquez. Sephard meant . . . well, Sephardic, and Moore . . . uh, Moor. The Kennedy name itself seemed to come from Turkish, designating someone connected with the "seat of the khan, or governor," as in Candy, the capital of Crete (now Irakleion).

There were yet other camps who looked at the same findings. Paul Heinegg, a retired engineer who studied free African Americans for many years, believed the Melungeons were examples of early colonial blacks able to marry white women and own land in a day before discrimination. Eloy Gallegos and Manuel Mira both wrote passionate books tracing Melungeons to the Portuguese colonists of St. Elena (a sixteenth-century fort near Beaufort, South Carolina). Adam Eterovich argued they were Croatians. Theories about Melungeons flew thick and fast all over the place.

Whether carried out professionally or conceived as an amateur DNA project, the Jones study and all others have been limited in one important respect. Only the Y chromosome or mitochondrial DNA testimony was looked into. The strict male and strict female lines are by no means the only ones in a family tree. Conventional DNA tests don't tell us anything about our mother's father or father's mother. If you go back ten generations, you have more than a thousand distinct lines. The old approach of genetic genealogy can target only two. Only recently has it become feasible to pry loose answers regarding all the in-between and hidden lines. Autosomal (non-sex-related) tests can look at markers scattered across a person's entire genome. These procedures can estimate your total ancestral contributions, as well as ethnic composition. They have expanded our picture of the human genetic past by leaps and bounds.

It was time to try the emerging technology on the mystery of the Melungeons. Hoping to succeed where others had failed, Beth Hirschman and I applied the new DNA fingerprint test to a small sample of self-identifying Melungeons. Like most other tests, the DNA fingerprint uses polymerase chain reaction chemistry to amplify a cheek-swab specimen produced by rubbing something like a Q-tip against the inside of your cheek and collecting buccal (pronounced "buckle") cells. The swabs are usually collected at home and sent back by mail to the lab. Technicians then extract your DNA. In this test, the markers discerned are not locations on the Y chromosome in the strict male line, nor are they mutations in the mitochondrial DNA of an ancient female lineage, but the loci used by forensic scientists to obtain a genetic identity profile and investigate crime scene evidence. Most of us are familiar with this DNA profile from television police shows. In a revolutionary application of this method of identification to ancestry, an individual's profile is put through special population frequency databases. A strong match with any population (say, France/Toulouse or Greek Cypriot or Apache) suggests you have ancestors from that part of the world. The DNA fingerprint test excels at finding small degrees of admixture and was perfect for our Melungeon survey. By evaluating the top matches for the group, we believed we might arrive at an overall ethnic profile for Melungeons, one showing what countries and parts of the world their ancestors came from and how much admixture they had from Native Americans and Africans.

All of our Melungeon volunteers had exclusively south central Appalachian ancestry over the past five generations and a surname from the list published in Brent Kennedy's book. Brent and his brother Richard both gave samples, as did our own two extended families. Having siblings, parents, children, aunts, uncles and others, we decided, would help validate the methodology. More than one participant was a repeat from the Jones study. Most were prominent in the Melungeon awareness movement. Wayne Winkler, the president of the Melungeon Heritage Association, joined the project, as did Nancy Sparks Morrison, founder of a Melungeon health information service on the Internet.

Analysis of the data dispels any notion that

Melungeons are ethnically non-diverse from the surrounding population or even homogenous among themselves. Melungeons are solidly distinct and highly diversified at the same time. Their most striking features are elevated Jewish, Middle Eastern, Native American, Sub-Saharan African and Iberian ancestry. All but two of the Melungeons in the study have a match with a Sephardic Jewish population as defined by the forensic team of Antonia Picornell. All have very strong to moderate Middle Eastern matches. One participant has high matches with every Middle Eastern population included in the database. Another Melungeon has Saudi Arabia at the top and Yemeni in second position. For both, likely ancestral places of origin are uniformly distributed throughout the Eastern Mediterranean, North Africa, the Arabian Peninsula and Iraq/Iran/Afghanistan, while Northern Europe is, to a greater or lesser degree, de-emphasized. This result graphically illustrates the fact that Melungeon ethnicity on average is more Mediterranean and "browner" than that of their overwhelmingly Northern European neighbors. DNA brings out the difference like night and day — or rather, olive and white.

The Kennedy brothers emerge with an Ashkenazic Jewish pattern. As outlined by Brent Kennedy in his book, they have a "family origin story" suggesting the possibility of Jewish ancestors, but the whisper was confirmed through genealogical research only in the past few years. DNA is no respecter of feelings. Again, it blurted out a secret that no amount of paper-driven research could expose. Genes trump genealogy. Indeed, Beth Hirschman's own pedigree on the face of it is linked to the illustrious Maryland Chases. Finding out that the Chase connection was manufactured to dodge racial prejudice and safeguard appearances launched her on her own journey toward discovering her true identity.

Native American matches appear in the profiles of all Melungeons according to the study. They are dominant in my own, Athabaskan Alaskan being No. 1, and ten out of twenty falling into the category. In my case, most of Northern Europe is, again, of lesser rank. Also, most of the Middle East is unimportant, the exception being the Jewish match brightly lit up in Israel on the map. When I learned of these matches, it meshed with my own prior understanding of my genealogy. In the study, the Native American Lumbee population of North Carolina registered as the top match for three Melungeons and was in second place for one other. The same result appeared in the lineup of one-fourth of all the participants. The Lumbee are often compared to Melungeons because of their mixed ancestry, marginalized history and unusual customs and traditions.

Like Native American and Middle Eastern, Sub-Saharan African admixture is an essential part of what it means to be Melungeon. Certain families such as the Goins, Collins and Driggers were either rumored to be black or confessed as much themselves. African matches had a strong showing in two-thirds of the individuals studied by us. Sub-Saharan African appears to be the overriding ancestry in at least two (although remember that matches cannot be equated with percentages). One of these, a Goins descendant, belonged to a "core" Melungeon family. Yet some Melungeons do not appear to have any indication of Sub-Saharan African heritage whatever. Sub-Saharan ancestry is thus relatively common, but not universal. Overall, the amount of admixture for both ethnicities is about the same as in the Jones study—5% Sub-Saharan African and 5% Native American.

Notable in the study was a low incidence of ancestry from England. This phenomenon can be glimpsed in the browning out of dots in Northwestern Europe. Matches to what the database defines as "Caucasian American" are few and far between. For some Melungeons, Sub-Saharan African, Middle Eastern, or North African ancestry evidently replaces Caucasian as the leading component of their ethnicity. Non-English looks, combined with a connection with Scottish, Irish and other minority cultures, evidently sealed Melungeons' fates in the eyes the English majority population around them.

Iberian ancestry outranks any other in Melungeons. Although it is something totally counter-intuitive, people who live in Kentucky and Tennessee and other Appalachian locations have a lot of Spanish, Portuguese, Latin American and Hispanic genes in them. One-third of our Melungeons emphasized these ethnicities in their overall makeup. This fits well with the abundance of Spanish and Portuguese surnames among Melungeon families. The modal, or most common, response in the study is Andalusia in the South of

Spain, a strongly Arab part of the country, and the last refuge of the Moors. Berber is another ethnicity that provides a common thread in Melungeon identity, as well as strong resonance in family histories. Moroccan and related North African populations are found at the top in several of our participants' profiles. Recall that some of the surnames regarded as Melungeon are quite literally Berber; about fifteen percent of all Sephardic Jewish surnames are too. The Berber element seems largely related to Andalusian ancestry, since following the conquest of Spain by Berber armies in 710, Andalusia became the Moorish stronghold.

Several other countries cropping up in the profiles are Turkey, Croatia, Serbia, Greece, Bosnia, Slovenia, Italy, and Poland. Except for Poland, all these lie within the Mediterranean orbit. Places like Livorno and Venice, Italy; Thessaloniki, Greece; and Izmir and Constantinople, Turkey were waystations in the diaspora of Sephardic Jews after their expulsion from Spain. Florida Atlantic University sociology professor Abraham Lavender believes this distribution of DNA reflects the very footsteps of Jews fleeing persecution throughout the early modern era, although he also raises the possibility that it represents a far more ancient pattern of Jewish populations.

What European countries emerge as important? Here again there are distinct answers. France exhibits the highest number of matches, with the South (Toulouse) exceeding the North (Lille). Notably, southern France experienced a large population influx from Spain and North Africa during the Middle Ages. Scotland is not far behind, however, and in fact, if we add together the two sub-populations of these countries, wins the top spot. The Northeast (Dundee) measurably surpasses the Southwest (Glasgow). This is consistent Hirschman's and my findings in *When Scotland Was Jewish* documenting a strong Sephardic/Moorish presence in northeastern Scotland following the Crusades. Melungeons seem to have far more Highlands than Lowlands kinsmen.

In conclusion, Melungeons have pre-dominantly northeastern Scottish ancestry along with southern European elements such as Portuguese and southern French. They exhibit less solidarity with the northwestern European countries adjacent to Scotland—England/Wales, Netherlands, Norway, Belgium, Denmark, neighbors that might be expected to figure more prominently in their mix—than they do to the Mediterranean lands. Whenever such an anomaly occurs, the explanation must lie in more than the straightforward, random expansion and blending of peoples. Population geneticists speak here of a non-starlike distribution pattern. Notably, northern Scotland, especially Aberdeen, had closer historical links with Poland and the Baltic than with, say, England. Scotland traditionally sought alliances with France, not England.

It seems that the isolation of Melungeons began before they arrived in the future United States. They brought over to the Appalachians an essentially disparate and distinct Scottish population. What they shared physically were, of course, darker coloring of their skin, hair and eyes and more exotic looks. On the English frontier, these traits set them apart from northwestern Europeans and led to their being branded "foreign," "colored" and "non-white."

It is easy to imagine that most of the original founding Melungeon foremothers and forefathers were not Christian. Native Americans, Berbers and Sub-Saharan Africans would have held religious beliefs of an animistic form, invoking solar, lunar, water, earth, fire and spiritual forces as well as natural calendric ceremonies. Arabic and Turkish-descended Melungeons probably probably imbibed a syncretistic blend of Sunni and Shi'ia traditions. Iberian and Polish/Balkan Jews blended their Sephardic and Ashkenazic religious practices. If South Asians were present in the early Melungeon settlements, they probably contributed Gypsy or Romani customs.

Autosomal DNA clearly shows that Colonial North America—at least in the southeastern region—was inhabited by a multi-ethnic, multi-religious population from its inception. There is an astonishing level of diversity buried in the hills of Kentucky and Tennessee.

"I should have known," I told Beth and my wife at the time all our lives took a sort of strange turn. "One grandmother was named Palestine and I had an uncle named Josephus." But why hadn't my family told me of this? When I confronted my mother, she said, "Well, what of it?" Teresa's experiences were similar. Her father admitted having been made to wear a yarmulke as a little boy, and having an aunt who sang "in the synagogue." Wondrous artifacts crept out of the closet—a silver menorah, letters between two great-granduncles calling each other Jews, whispers of free loans from a bank run by relatives . . . . Now suddenly Jewish, we ventured on a tour of Mickve Israel in Savannah, North America's third oldest Jewish congregation. There we met Rabbi Arnold Belzer. He knew of the Melungeons and had heard similar tales about crypto-Jewish families. "You can't convert to Judaism," he explained. "You can only return." He told us that Bevis Marks Synagogue was first built in London in 1703. He was just then about to embark on a trip to attend its 300th anniversary. Spanish and Portuguese crypto-Jews returned there to Judaism after as long a lapse as four hundred years. So we returned.

Modern genetics often have a deep influence on people's lives. Giving up the teaching profession, I founded a DNA testing company, DNA Consultants. Few customers, I learned, could easily dismiss the results of a DNA test once that step was taken. Those for whom it became a life-altering event are more common than the opposite. Customers' testimony to the uncanny truth of DNA poured in on all sides. Fellow Melungeons were particularly grateful for answers to the longstanding questions in their lives.

Richard Stewart in West Virginia wrote, "I was always told that we were Scottish, English, Irish. Now I know I have more Southeastern Europe (Turkey) and Middle Eastern (Jewish) ancestry than I do in Northern Europe."

Julia Starnes, whose mother and father's DNA happened to have a significant amount of Middle

Eastern though they were sixth generation East Tennesseans, told a Melungeon discussion board:

What I find personally interesting is that for seven years I have been studying dances of the Middle East, Spain, Turkey, and most recently India — following the Romani trail. I have a particular passion for the music and dance of the Turkish Romani.... It took very little for me to become attuned to the instrumentation and rhythms associated with the music of these countries.... Maybe I'm just being silly, but I feel that the Romani music especially speaks to my heart and soul. I feel that I perform at my best when picking music from the regions that are connected to my genetic (though not cultural) heritage.

Bowled over by Spanish, Portuguese and Latin American matches, another test taker wondered, "Ethically and legally, on a census or job form that asks for racial identity, should I now be filling out Hispanic instead of Caucasian?"

Nancy Sparks Morrison, who runs the Melungeon Health discussion list, passes on story after story from those who benefited from a DNA analysis by being better able to accept or manage their health. One Appalachian native finally got her doctor to diagnose her with familial Mediterranean fever and prescribe the drug colchicine after bringing in an ancestry report demonstrating she had genetic forbears in Turkey and the Eastern Mediterranean. The family practitioner knew very little about the disease, which was clinically unreported previously in Tennessee.

The opportunities to learn from DNA are especially rife for adopted children who do not know their biological parents or ethnic background. It is estimated as many as fifteen percent of Americans are either adopted or descended from an adopted person. I will let one of these—or rather her adoptive sister—tell in her own words what taking a DNA test did for them.

When Tina was given up for adoption, all information about her birth father was provided by her birth mother, who was Caucasian of Czechoslovakian/ German heritage and stated the father was very light-skinned African American. The last dozen years or so, Tina has questioned her ethnicity. She has been asked repeatedly if she is African American, Ethiopian, Jamaican, Latin of various types, East Indian, Middle Eastern, Jewish, Greek, or Armenian. Some people have said she looks Russian, Native American Indian, Hawaiian or even Asian!

Tina's report showed Hispanic (Spanish/ Portuguese) and Scottish/English/Welsh with Middle Eastern and American Indian admixture. Also, it said, there may be Slovenian/Polish/Gypsy . . . with a medium match to Sephardic Jews. There was no Sub-Saharan African or East Asian. Her deep ancestry was all Mediterranean, North African Arab and/or Berber, Portuguese and Middle Eastern. In my own ignorance, I had not realized that other groups of people also had her markedly curly hair. It was so much fun finding pictures of Berber/North African Arabs with my sister's hair and nose.

Tina is delighted with her Mediterranean and Middle Eastern roots . . . . She was not as surprised as I was. It is as if her spirit bore witness to the truth for years before this testing was even possible. It settled her . . . . It gives her a settled identity, not a presumed identity. It has opened my eyes to the beauty of many people in the world I had never paid attention to before.

If DNA is a hobby, it is a serious one. It is not a quest that should be entered upon just for fun. The most fulfilling aspect of DNA testing for me personally and professionally has been to see the effect it has had in opening up an interest in other peoples and countries. By revealing the interrelatedness of us all, DNA can not only give new meaning and depth to self-identity but also play an important part in fostering peace, tolerance and understanding around the world.

Oddly, our church had a star of David

2 DON QUIXOTE AND SENOR EGGPLANT

What exactly the word Melungeon means, where it comes from and to whom it is properly to be applied are topics that have been hotly debated without any definite conclusion having been reached. Even the language from which the term is derived is uncertain. Cases have been made for French, Turkish, Arabic and others. As a proper noun Melungeon is generally taken to refer to a descendant of a mixed people who lived at one time in the lower Appalachians. Genealogists are split between allotting these people a special status and consigning them ordinary, run-of-the-mill backgrounds in British frontier families. It is claimed that some carried sub-Saharan and American Indian genes, while it is also vehemently asserted that most did not. Whatever the reasons, Melungeons were ostracized and marginalized, beginning in the eighteenth century. That they were simply an element in society that fell on hard times was a theory first proposed by Bureau of Inidan Affairs careerist Virginia DeMarce in 1992. Her article in the *National Genealogical Society Quarterly* was titled "Verry Slitly Mixt': Tri-Racial Isolate Families of the Upper South - A Genealogical Study." The "status apart" school of thought was championed by author Brent Kennedy, whose fundamental and far-reaching study appeared in 1994.

Kennedy's research was corroborated by numerous scholarly and popular works over the next decade, including the ethnic identity contributions of Rutgers University marketing professor Elizabeth C. Hirschman. An article on Melungeon DNA by myself (Yates) and Hirschman appeared in *Appalachian Journal* in 2010 and seemed to prove from a genetic, if not genealogical perspective, that a core component of historical Melungeons were Sephardic Jews, a persecuted religious minority similar to the crypto-Jews of New Mexico. If we dig into the history of the controversy, we see that it goes back at least to Edward T. Price in the *Annals of the Association of American Geographers*, who identified Melungeons as a "white-Negro-Indian racial mixture in the Eastern United States." Discussions on the Internet usually argue for and against Price's definition and attempt to make adjustments to it but few people change the grounds of the argument. Some adherents of the "just plain folks" approach pointedly ignore Kennedy and Hirschman's Jewish, Turkish and Middle Eastern proposals.

The *Dictionary of American Regional English* defines Melungeon as "a member of a racially mixed group of people centered in northeastern Tennessee and southwestern Virginia." That much seems safe and unremarkable, although some have questioned whether Melungeons can be categorically distinguished from their neighbors by either ethnic composition or social criteria.

As to the etymology and original usage of the term, several very different theories have been advanced. Melungeon health researcher Nancy Morrison lists seven etymologies suggested over the years: 1) a connection to Angolan tribes called the Malungu, 2) the Turkish phrase *melun çan* (pronounced muh-LUNGE-uhn), meaning "lost soul," 3) a hypothetical word Malengine, "evil machination," since "some Melungeons were known to be 'tricky,'" 4) an Afro-Portuguese word *melungo*, meaning shipmate, 5) French *mélange* "mixed," 6) French *melongène* "eggplant," in reference to the dark skin of Melungeons, and 7) a word in the Croatian language stemming from the passengers of five ships landing in the Carolinas in 1449 (Louis Adamic). The two most widely accepted of these explanations seem to be that the word is "perhaps" based on French *mélange,* mixture, crossing of races—the view of most reference works—and that it is derived from Turkish *melun çan*, meaning "**cursed soul.**" The latter is the one popularized and personally endorsed by Kennedy.

But there is a minority opinion. The word Melungeon is phonetically identical to melongen(a), an obsolete Latinate word for eggplant that fell out of favor as the common term for eggplant during the nineteenth century. The English word is related to *melanzana* (or *mulenyam* or *molonjohn*), a slang expression for eggplant used by Italian Americans as a slur for black persons. The term crops up, for instance, in the recent popular television series *The Sopranos*, and Melungeon researchers Mike Nassau, Charles Everett and Manuel Mira had previously drawn attention to it.

Before proceeding to our reasons for embracing such an etymology, let us first examine the two derivations that until now have been leading contenders, French mélange and Turkish *melun çan*. Neither of these, alas, are supported by a paper trail or oral tradition. Kennedy's "cursed souls" resonates with many people who have Melungeon roots or connections, and it seems to be vindicated by certain scholars from Turkey and the Arabic-speaking world whom Kennedy has consulted. Yet no use of *melun çan* paralleling "Melungeon" in Turkish or Arabic sources can be actually documented. No person claiming Melungeon ancestry or labeled as Melungeon appears to have spoken or have been acquainted with these languages before the publication of Kennedy's book.

By the same token, few considerations other than a superficial resemblance have been put forth why "mélange" should be accepted as the real story behind the word. French was hardly spoken in the Melungeon heartland. Although Charles Everett published an essay in *Appalachian Journal* citing the existence of French settlers in southwest

Virginia beginning in the 1790s, it does not follow that a foreign coinage of this sort would have passed into general usage from such a small group, nor that it would then have been been applied to a non-French minority by the non-French majority. The French have other words for people of mixed blood — metis and creole come to mind. If the intent was to denote someone as "mixed" in the sense of a mélange of ancestry, it seems there were already many ways to say this without inventing a new word. A word with the force of "mixt 'uns" is in no French dictionary today. It is less than likely that people in the English-speaking colonies or early United States would have designated members of *any* group with such an expression.

The law of simple explanations works against both these candidates. An English origin must naturally carry more weight than the others. We thus believe that Melungeon comes from melongen, and that the two sound-alikes are linked historically in connotation and usage.

As a starting point, let us list chronologically the appearances of the word Melungeon in print. Observe the variations in spelling.

1810 'Lungeons. "foreigners . . . men of mystery . . . neither Negro nor Indian." A memoir by pioneer Jacob Mooney from Baxter County, Arkansas Centennial History (1972).

Melungins. "....she harbored them Melungins." Stony Creek Baptist Church Minutes, Washington County, Virginia

Malungeon. "An impudent Malungeon. . . half Negro and half Indian...lived in a delightful Utopia of their own creation, trampling on the marriage relation, despising all forms of religion...intermixed with the Indians." — *Brownlow's Whig*, Jonesboro, Tenn.

1848 Melungen. Village at Blackwater Creek in Hancock Co. — *Knoxville (Tenn.) Register*.

1849 "A singular species of the human animal called Melungens." — *Littell's Magazine.*

Malungens. "interesting gentlemen—and no 'malungens'." — *Bluegrass Confederate: The Headquarters Diary of Edward O. Guerrant.*

1864 Malungeon. "Bushwackers." —Battles and Sketches of the Army of Tennessee.

1873 Malunjins. "Known by the local name of 'Malunjins' are a mixture of whites, blacks and Indians...are now engaged in illicit distilling and other lawless pursuits." — *The Republic: A Monthly Magazine.*

1875 Malungens. "He was a small spare made man, with low, flat head, had a dark complexion, rather a flat nose, turned up at the end. He wore his hair short, and it was always inclined to curl or kink . . . mixed blood people." —Trial of Solomon Bolton descendants, or Lewis Shepherd case in Hamilton Co., Tenn.

1886 "A peculiar admixture of white and Indian blood." —Goodspeed's *History of Tennessee.*

1889 Melungeons. A term "given to them by the whites, and proudly called themselves Portuguese." —Swan M. Burnett, "A note on the Melungeons," *American Anthropologist*.

1889 Melungeons. "This small peculiar race." —*Atlanta Constitution.*

1890 Melungeons, 'lungens'. "A branch of the Croatan tribe . . . in east Tennessee." — *The Knoxville Journal.*

1890 "From history we get nothing; not so much as the name, — Malungeons . . claimed to be Portuguese." — Will Allen Dromgoole, articles in *Boston Arena.*

1897 Melungeons. "Resented the appellation." — McDonald Furman in a S.C. newspaper article.

1900 Malungeons. — Otis.

1902 Malungeons. — Saturday Evening Post.

1903 "Derisively dubbed with the name 'Malungeons'." — Lewis M. Jarvis interview, *Sneedville (Tenn.) Times.*

1913 Melungeons. Most extensive study yet in *A History of Tennessee and Tennesseans* by Will T. Hale (Chicago: Lewis). "Their very name is a corruption of some foreign word unknown to them or to the few who have given them any study."

1914 Malungeons. — Wilson.

1940 "It was hard for a Melongeon in the world." — *Southern Literary Messenger*, Richmond, Va.

1947 Malungeon. "Nobody is entirely sure what the word is." — William L. Worden, "Sons of the Legend," *Saturday Evening Post.*

1966 Melungeon. Same as Free Person of Color. — Henry R. Price, "Melungeons: The Vanishing Colony of Newman's Ridge," paper at Tennessee Technological University, Cookeville, Tenn.

Although the term is hardly spelled the same twice, several conclusions can be drawn about it. Generally speaking, pronunciation seems to vacillate between a first syllable of Mel and Mal, a middle syllable of -un- and -on- and an ending in -geon, -jin, -gen and -gin. In speech it is apparently stressed on the second syllable, a pronunciation which may explain the form 'Lungeons. Are these orthographic variations erratic or is there something we can learn from them? The first literate use occurs in the transcribed minutes of a Primitive Baptist church in Hancock County, Tennessee, where the word is spelled *Melungin*. Wherever else the argument may take us, keep this form in mind. The Mel- spelling eventually prevails; it has the greatest title to being the "authentic" one. Littell's Magazine represents the first use of the word in actual print, giving it as *Malungen*. We can regard that renderi of the ending as a better one than the colloquial *-eon* which became popular in and after the Civil War, and which was repeated and perpetuated by ethnographers and anthropologists. In short, the form *Melungin* in the church minutes of 1813 has the ring of truth. With allowance made for Southern regional pronunciation of *i* for *e* and scribal vagaries, the intended form could well have been *Melongen* — good, old-fashioned English melongen or melongena.

As for the word's meaning, its first appearance bears careful scrutiny and analysis:

September the 26, 1813

Church sat in love. Brother Kilgore, Moderator. Then came forward Sister [Jean] Kitchen and complained to the church against Susanna Stallard for saying she harbored them Melungins. Sister Sook [Stallard] said she was hurt with her for believing her child [Sarah Kitchen?] and not believing her, and she won't talk to her to get satisfaction, and both is "pigedish" ["piggedish," pig-headed], one against the other. Sister Sook lays it down and the church forgives her....

A critical exposition seems in order because this crucial passage has often been misread. The pronoun references in it have frequently been misconstrued. To expound, the passage tells of a misunderstanding between two women in the congregation of a church. The context is a religious one. Jean Kitchen complains that Susanna Stallard is going around saying behind her back that she (Jean Kitchen) is "harboring" Melungeons. Susanna (called Sook for short) replies that this is only what Jean's daughter Sarah says and Jean should have asked *her* (Susanna Stallard) about it. "Them Melungins" has an obvious contemptuous or derogatory force. "Harbor" is a word one might expect to be applied to runaway slaves or fugitives from justice, although it could also have described simply a situation in which Sister Stallard rightly or wrongly suspected Sister Kitchen of concealing people who were just not considered good society or proper associates in the eyes of the church. Do the facts claimed by Jean Kitchen in her defense mean that Sister Kitchen was not hiding anyone at all, or that the persons she was hiding were not of the "Melungeon" persuasion? Or was it all nothing but senseless gossip? Were the two women arguing about semantics? We will probably never know for sure. The affronted party Susanna Stallard "lays it down," and the two congregants make peace.

Whatever the full meaning is of this offhand remark about "Melungins," it is apparent that the term functions as a slur of some sort. It presses some hot buttons. Everett, among others, was not unaware of the name calling, although he believes the "Melungins" were "excommunicated" from the church because they were French settlers from nearby Fort Blackmore. They were thus branded "mixtures" in their own language. We believe there is more to the story, however.

From its spotty first appearances, the word Melungeon embarked on a checkered career in the East Tennessee press. We catch mentions and allusions for about half a century before the slur (along with, presumably, the people it references) falls off in frequency and the record becomes silent. In the second half of the twentieth century, Melungeon passes into an enigmatic archaism. The most common adjective associated with the word is probably "mysterious." In the meantime, from about the 1880s, ethnographers and anthropologists like James Mooney of the Smithsonian extend Melungeon identity to Redbones, Carolina Turks, Lumbees, Croatan Indians and other groups. From being narrowly applied to residents of Hancock County, Tennessee, especially certain families on Newmans Ridge, the term takes on a catch-all meaning of "persons of color." Such may or may not have been the thrust of the original word.

Whatever else we can conclude by sifting the evidence, it is clear the term Melungeons was a label imposed upon them by society. They did not use the term of themselves; it is not an ethnonym. As averred of the heroine of "Sons of the Legend," a magazine piece about a Melungeon woman, "one word she will never say [is] 'Malungeon'." In short, it was a derogatory name with racial overtones. Only after Brent Kennedy's book (whose subtitle was *Resurrection of a Proud Legacy*) did the word start to undergo an about-face. People began to use it as a self-identifier. It became a badge of honor, no longer a stigma. There was now a Melungeon Movement, Melungeon website and Melungeon Registry. By 2007, Melungeon identity was a desirable cultural commodity. It became the subject of a consumer identity study by Elizabeth Hirschman, a specialist in the intersection between ethnicity or culture and marketing strategies. Lisa Alther, a Kingsport, Tennessee native who rediscovered her Melungeon roots, came out with the best-selling novel *Kinfolks* in the same year.

The word *Melungin* used by Sister Kitchen is exactly the same as a then-common name for eggplants. The English word long in currency both in writing and speech for eggplant was *melongen(a)*. Albeit old-fashioned, even in the nineteenth century, melongen *is* an English word, not French, Turkish or German. Although exotic and foreign-sounding, it would certainly have been understood by the English-speaking members of the Stony Creek Church in the sense of "eggplant." Until about the mid-nineteenth century, when it was replaced by "eggplant," it was the pervasive and typical term for the plant and its fruit. For example, melongena was the term employed in gardening manuals like Philip Miller's *The Gardeners Dictionary* (1735). It appeared in the form melongen in literary compositions, such as an adaptation of the Arab poet Al-Mutannabi (1819), where the

Arab poet describes a hawk's eye as "black and beautiful as a black melongen." Unquestionably, Sister Kitchens and her co-religionists knew that "them Melungins" meant "those Melongens," and that "those Melongens" referred to "those Eggplants."

Incidentally, the word melongen(a) was pronounced in English both with a hard and soft *g*, as has been true also of the word Melungeon. And like Melungeon, melongen is stressed on the second syllable. Tellingly, among its many now-obsolete synonyms are Jew's apple and apple of scorn, further evidence of its history as a slur. *Mala* "apple" (in Latin and Italian) is perhaps the influence behind an occasional spelling of both melongen and Melungeons with *mal-* instead of *mel-*, even though the ultimate source of melongen(a) is not Latin or Italian, but Arabic.

A brief sketch of eggplants and the various names that have been used for them takes us all over the world. One authority has written that "probably there is no word of the kind which has undergone such extraordinary variety of modifications, whilst retaining the same meaning, as this." Another observes, "The literature contains many names for eggplant, due to the many appellations in its home country (India), the number of countries where grown, together with the transliteration difficulties from one language to another." The eggplant originated in northeastern India, Burma or northern Thailand, and has been known to the people of that region for about 2,000 years. Sanskrit names are *vartta, varttaka, vaatinga* or *bhantaaki,* and *badanjan* or *bungan*. The last-mentioned variants passed into Persian as *baadangan, baatangaan, badenjan* and then into Arabic as *bedengiam, bedengaim, badindjan, baadanjaan* and *melongena*. From Arab lands the eggplant reached other countries around the Mediterranean. It was called *patlidjan* in Turkish, *tabendjalts* in Berber languages in North Africa, *beringela* in Portuguese, *berengena* in Spanish, *bérengène* and *aubergine* in French, *brinjal* in India (via a re-introduction by the Portuguese) and, again, *bringelle* in France. People gave different varieties different names, often distinguishing between annual eggplants and perennial ones, those with and without spines, black ones versus white, lilac, yellow and brown, ornamental as opposed to edible, and sizes and shapes ranging from pear-shaped to large oblong melon-like fruits.

All these names are ultimately derived from the same root. In the eighteenth century, Linnaeus chose Melongena as the scientific name, and this became the vernacular name in English and Dutch. Medieval and Late Latin forms were *melongiane, melongiana* and *melonge*. Forms of the word in other European languages are Dutch *melongaena, melanzan, melanzaan* (1847), French *melongène, melongine, melongene*, Greek *melitzane*, German *melongena* and Italian *melanzana*. There are similar variants in Catalan, Spanish, Portuguese, Swedish, Danish, Polish and even Esperanto. Not until the British occupation of India in the eighteenth century did "melongenas" begin to be called "eggplants" instead. Underlying a shift in preferential usage was that the small white ornamental variety grown in northern Europe resembled eggs (German *Eierfrucht*). Since then, the British continued to use the older French culinary term, aubergine, while Americans came to favor "eggplant." In sum, Melongen(a) and Melungeon have an ancient pedigree.

The switch from "melongena" to "eggplant" corresponded in non-Mediterranean countries like England and America to gradual acceptance of the plant as an edible one, and to its transformation from a showy ornamental into an easily-grown staple for the dinnertable. Like tomatoes, eggplants belong to the deadly nightshade family. For centuries they were deemed poisonous. In being introduced in Christian lands, the eggplant acquired a reputation as a magical plant similar to the mandrake, which allegedly possessed a poison with stupor-causing, aphrodisiacal and madness-inducing effects. Some of the melongena's alternative names, historically, are apples of love, apples of Sodom, love-apple, mad-apple (*mala insana* or *melanzana* in Italian) and raging apple. It has been called Jew's apple since about 1580. This was a year, coincidentally, that saw the mass flight of Jews from Portugal as that country was united under one crown with Spain and the Spanish Inquisition was extended to Portugal with full civil powers. Many of these new exiles went to the Dutch Republic, which declared its independence from Spain, July 26, 1581. It was the beginning of the golden age of Sephardic Jews abroad.

Eggplant did not thrive in northern climates. It was best suited to Spain, Italy, Israel, Turkey and Egypt, where it grew wild. Wherever Arabs and Jews went, there also followed the lowly eggplant.

Arabs introduced it to North Africa, Spain and Sicily. After their 1492 expulsion from Spain, Jews took it with them into exile — to Sicily, where it was adopted to make eggplant Parmigiana, Greece (whence mousaka) and even the Netherlands and British Isles. Sephardic Jews introduced it to Brazil, the Caribbean and the Carolinas beginning in the seventeenth century. According to an English author in 1735, "These Plants are greatly cultivated in the Gardens of Italy, Spain and Barbary, in which Places the Inhabitants eat the Fruit of them, [but] these Plants are only preserv'd as Curiosities in the English Gardens, the Fruit being never us'd in this Country, except by some Italians or Spaniards, who have been accustom'd to eat of them in their own Countries." The eggplant was regarded as exotic in northern Europe, reminding people especially of Spaniards and Portuguese. "In Europe, it was well understood that eggplant was of foreign origin." Such associations are evidently in the background of the remarks in our church minutes. By referring to the suspicious guests her fellow congregant was "harboring" as "Them Eggplants," Sister Stallard may as well have said "Them Foreigners."

Eggplant entered the Iberian Peninsula as early as the eighth century with the conquering Arabs and their Berber army. It is recorded as a favorite dish there by the twelfth century. Under the Mamluks and during the period of the Crusades, it is mentioned as one of the crops grown in the land of Israel. There was an annual variety in addition to a spiny semi-annual one. "This difference fueled a Jewish legal controversy as to whether eggplant was a vegetable or the fruit of a tree." If produce of a tree, eggplant belonged to those special fruits eaten by the faithful during Passover such as almonds, dates, pomegranates, pears and peaches. Eggplant salad rapidly rose to be a staple Sabbath dish because it required little work and could be prepared the day before. In fact, eggplant became so popular among Jews that "there is a saying of the eggplant that there are so many different ways of preparing it that if during the eggplant season a woman says to her husband, 'I know not what to provide for dinner,' he has sufficient cause for divorcing her."

"What is crystal clear," accord to Judaic scholar David Gitlitz, "is that in Iberia the eggplant was closely associated with Semitic cultures" (*A Drizzle of Honey. The Lives and Recipes of Spain's Secret Jews*). As early as the thirteenth century, the *Al-Andalus* cookbook contained a recipe called "Eggplant Jewish Style." In the early fifteenth century, shortly after Jews in the Peninsula began to be forced to convert to Christianity, eggplant eater was a calling word for a secret Jew or hypocritical New Christian. Writes Spanish literary scholar David Nirenberg: "It was not until the 1430s that we start to find widespread evidence of skepticism about the Christianity of the converts and widespread efforts to 'rejudaise' them." He notes that the first literary representations of *converso* Jewishness appear in the *Cancionero de Baena*, an anthology of court verse compiled by Juan Alfonso de Baena in Castile. In the manner of classical Arabic, these compositions alternated between praise and invective. "Prominent among the charges they hurl is the accusation of Jewishness." Each vying to be more unctuous than the previous, the poets even accuse their noble host Juan Alfonso of being secretly Jewish. They claim his birthplace is a land where "much good eggplant" is grown, and that he has "eyes of eggplant."

Anything that smacked of eggplant conveyed a strong hint of Jewishness. And it would only be a short step for eggplant to take on anti-Semitic overtones.

A poem written in the latter part of the fifteenth century by Rodrigo de Cota tells how friends and family were served eggplant at a *converso* wedding. His *Epitalamio burlesco* lambasts the gentile guests who attend the wedding of the grandson of Diego Arias Dávila. The latter was finance minister for King Enrique IV of Castile. De Cota happened not to be invited to the illustrious affair and vents his disgruntlement by satirizing the Christian customs of the guests, most of whom were, like him, thinly disguised Jews.

> *At this Jewish wedding party*
> *bristly pig was not consumed;*
> *not one single scaleless fish*
> *went down the gullet of the groom;*
> *instead, an eggplant casserole*
> *with saffron and Swiss chard;*
> *and whoever swore by "Jesus"*
> *from the meatball pot was barred.*

Gitlitz and Davidson give the recipe in their book *A Drizzle of Honey*.

Eggplant stew was so firmly linked by now with crypto-Jewish behavior that when the *converso* poet Juan de Valladolid kissed the silver tray used at mass to carry the consecrated host, "it miraculously turned into an eggplant stew. "The event was reported in a satire by the Count of Paredes, viceroy of New Spain (1638-1692), who was suspected of having pro-*converso* leanings. The records of the Spanish Inquisition contain several cases of New Christians and *conversos* running afoul of the authorities by preferring Jewish eggplant to Christian pork. Officials sometimes staged public spectacles in which arrested or suspected Judaizers were forced to consume pork as a test of faith.

Two Inquisition cases from the sixteenth century are especially instructive for us. In one, María González, wife of Pedro de Villarreal, gives an affidavit to Inquisitors about the secret Jewish ceremonies and customs of her friends and neighbors. Among the information she divulges is that on one Sabbath afternoon when she was visiting in the home of Ximon de la Çarça, she came upon his wife, Catalina de Teva, with other ladies dressed in their finest clothes eating an eggplant casserole they had prepared the night before. In another case, the Ciudad Real Tribunal reopens charges of judaizing against Beatriz and Isabel González, daughters of the prominent citizen Fernán González. Officials previously convicted them of koshering their meat, dressing up for the Sabbath, lighting candles and celebrating Yom Kippur and Passover, but the charges were dismissed because of their youth. Now the two sisters are summoned again to answer for their damning behavior. When they get wind of the tribunal's intent, however, they flee to Portugal, where many of their fellow Jews found refuge under Manuel I. The Inquisitors now subpoena a servant, Catalina Martín, and try Beatriz and Isabel in absentia. The servant verifies the whole family's Jewish practices. She deposes to the authorities that the two sisters "used to pray, their shoulders covered with linen cloths, lowering and raising their heads and swaying forward and backward." She also sets down Beatriz and Isabel González' recipe for Sabbath eggplant casserole for all posterity. It featured onions, chicken soup, cinnamon, cardamom, coriander, cilantro and cloves.

The use of eggplants to stigmatize Jews survives even down to the present. Critic Edward Said portrays in one of his writings a shifty lawyer called Isam al-Bathanjani (Isam the Eggplant). The Spanish poet-novelist Juan Goytisolo (born 1931) resurrects the figure of Cide Hamete Benengali—a reference to Miguel Cervantes' *Don Quixote.*

An understanding of eggplant allusions is central to *Don Quixote*. According to Cervantes, one day in Alcaná market in Toledo, a young boy was hawking old manuscripts and scraps of paper to a silk merchant when the author happened to come along. Seeking a continuation to the first volume of a book he had read on the adventures of Don Quixote he snatches up one of the volumes the youngster displayed and sees it is written in Arabic characters. Looking around for a Jew or Morisco to translate for him, he learns the volume is titled "History of Don Quixote of La Mancha, written by Cide Hamete Benengeli, an Arab historian." The invention of such a fantastic pedigree for a phantom source serves Cervantes well, for it allows him to create a mega-text embracing all of Spanish history and culture. *Don Quixote* is a parable for the lost world of Spain's celebrated *convivencia*, a flourishing period of coexistence between Arabs, Christians and Jews that ground to an abrupt end in 1492. Its death throes were echoed in the final extradition of the last Moors in Cervantes' own day. Clearly, Benengeli was an alter ego for Spain's epic romancer. Cervantes sympathized with Jews and Arabs and he probably came himself from a family of *conversos*.

Later in *Don Quixote* (Second Part, chapter II), the knight's sidekick Sancho Pancho, who has an unconscious knack for comical double entendres, bungles Benengeli's name, calling him Berenjena, Spanish for eggplant. In his characteristically zany manner, he patters on:

"Last night Bartolomé Carrasco's son . . . told me that the history of your grace is already in books, and it's called *The Ingenious Gentleman Don Quixote of La Mancha*; and he says that in it they mention me, Sancho Panza, by name, and my lady Dulcinea of Toboso [*for Toloso*], and other things that happened when we were alone, so that I crossed myself in fear at how the historian who wrote them could have known about them."

"I assure you, Sancho," said Don Quixote, "that the author of our history must be some wise enchanter, for nothing is hidden from them if they wish to write about it."

"Well," said Sancho, "if he was wise and an enchanter, then how is it possible . . . that the author of the history is named Cide Hamete Berenjena?"

"That is a Moorish name," responded Don Quixote.

"It must be," responded Sancho, "because I've heard that most Moors are very fond of eggplant."

"You must be mistaken, Sancho," said Don Quixote, "in the last name of this Cide, which in Arabic means *señor.*"

Sancho Panchez has learned there is a book in circulation telling about his master's adventures. He wonders how the author of the book could have known about them in detail without being a magician. His name, he remembers, was Cide Hamete Berenjena. Don Quixote confirms that the author must be a sorcerer because the name is Moorish, and his sidekick says, yes, and it means eggplant—a confused allusion to the witchcraft of "apples of Satan" or "mad apples." This is denied by Don Quixote, who maintains in a non sequitur that the name cannot be "eggplant" since Cide means Sir or Mr. To have the name Mr. Eggplant would be absurd.

Possibly, Sancho Panchez also knew that *berenjenero* ("one having the attributes of an eggplant") was a nickname for the inhabitants of Toledo, a center of Spanish Jewry and Moorish culture. At any rate, some critics have rationalized his slip of the tongue and argued that Arabic *benengeli* is indeed the same as Spanish *berenjenai,* and that both words designate eggplants. Others like Cervantist and Arabist Luce Lopez Baralt favor an etymology of *benengeli* in "son of an angel," tracing its pronunciation to Algeria, where

Cervantes lived for five years as a captive. The word probably functions on several levels, like most of Cervantes' puns. The philosopher Miguel de Unamuno proposed that the shadowy Benengeli depicted a Moroccan Jew.

There are modern instances of Jews named after the eggplant. Historically, eggplant served as such a telltale sign of Judaism that many Jews either adopted it as a surname or received it as a name from Christian officials. Thus we find Patlazhan (Hebrew for eggplant) in Kiev, Erenfrukt or Erifrukht (Yiddish), Aubergine in England, Melanzana in Italy and Melongen, Malungen and Melungen in American emigrants in Tennessee, Missouri and Ohio. There is even an L. Eggplant listed in the white pages of the Asheville, North Carolina telephone book. Could this be the origin of the Benenhaleys, a mixed blood family of the early Carolinas whose name is pronounced exactly the same as Arabic/Spanish *benengeli*? Like the Oxendines, Braveboys and certain other Sumter Turk families, the Benenhaleys have long puzzled genealogists.

How did "eggplant" come to be Italian slang for a black person? The surprising answer has little to do with the vegetable's color, since there were just as many eggplant varieties that were white in the past as purplish-black. As the following informal survey suggests, words such as *melanzana* and the dialectical form *mulignan* were not applied to Africans at first, but to certain dark-skinned Italians—Sicilians, South Italians and Spanish-Portuguese Jews. All were believed to have Sub-Saharan African blood, as, indeed, DNA studies today have confirmed about certain ethnic groups originating in South Mediterranean. More important, however, may have been the stigma of being outsiders, members of a non-Christian minority. Religious discrimination was more consequential than racial prejudice in those times. Only with emigrant Italian-Americans in the late nineteenth and twentieth centuries did the slur begin to be attached exclusively to African Americans.

Although Arabs introduced the eggplant to Sicily and southern Italy when they conquered the region in the eighth century, apparently it was not until the Sephardim settled in and passed on through Sicily that eggplants were spread to the rest of the country. The Kingdom of the Two Sicilys was intermittently part of the Spanish Empire. According to one account in the *Jewish Chronicle* in 2008, it was Jews expelled from southern Italy in the 1500s who introduced the eggplant to Rome, Florence, Venice and other cities to the north. This occurred during the years when various city-states and duchies offered refuge. A Sephardic Jewish physician residing in Ferrara, Antonius Musa Brasavolus (1500-1555), observed the eggplant's use by "certain sojourners from Spain," and commended it as a dish, taking pains to dispel the myth of its harmfulness and establish its acceptance as a food plant:

"We were aware, in summertime and for successive years, of the use of this melanzana apple by the noble ladies, Isabella and Julia of Tarragon. It was sometimes stewed, sometimes fried, with seasoning of oil, salt, pepper, and occasionally vinegar, and these ladies, so far from becoming insane, grew wiser with the passing time. Nor did I abstain from eating it; for these selfsame illustrious sisters were accustomed now and again to send portions of it, prepared as I have said, to my table during the time of their temporary abiding at Ferrara."

By the year 1570, eggplant had made its way onto a menu presented to Pope Pius V, where it was married with various exotic spices in a sauce accompanying fried veal liver and sweetbreads. The Tuscans called it *petronciane*, the Neapolitans *molegnano* (which was to morph into Italian-Americans' *mulignan*, abbreviated *mool* and *molonjohn*) and the Romans *marignani* (a conflation with *Marreno*?). In the late eighteenth century, the Scottish physician-author Tobias Smollett wrote of an Italian dish "made of the badenjean, which the Spaniards call berengena: it is much eaten in Spain and the Levant, as well as by the Moors in Barbary." He added, "This fruit is called *Melanzana* in Italy and is much esteemed by the Jews in Leghorn." Ever his bilious self, he finished by saying "it is at best an insipid dish."

From this survey we can see how the eggplant, complete with all its rich lore, spread to other parts of Europe with Sephardic Jews fleeing the Inquisition. Jews brought it to America from England, where the name was melongen. Identified with eggplants in the popular imagination as well as in the minds of civil and religious authorities, Jews had "eggplant" applied to them as an ethnic slur. It was a word fraught with historical meanings and associations, with legal and literary connotations. Its use was, as we might say today, loaded, much more than, say, the expression "garlic-head," sometimes heard of Italians. Acting in the manner of other deep-seated and unthinking epithets, it branded Jews as foreign, dark, sinister, transient, suspicious, heretical, unchristian, furtive, dissembling, secretive, deceitful, treacherous, malicious, materialistic, luxury loving — stereotypes Jews have ever and always been subjected to. It is was no accident that Primitive Baptists on the Appalachian frontier in 1813 were horrified to think that one of their members might be "harboring Melungeons." Would they have said "harboring" if Sister Kitchen had people of mixed blood, or of backward origins, or of uncouth manners in her house? No.

From evoking a Portuguese Jew, with overtones of crypto-Jew or secret Jew, the word Melungeon went on to designate the mixed Jewish, black and American Indian families who lived marginalized lives ·in places including, but not restricted to, Newmans Ridge. In a later chapter, we will see how a leading member of Sister Stallard and Sister Kitchens' community carried the term with him when he migrated to Arkansas and established a new Stony Creek Baptist Church in the West. Gradually, however, the original meaning and applications of the term were lost. Use of the word melongen in general society began to be replaced by that of "eggplant." Many of the Jewish families who settled in the Appalachians assimilated into the surrounding predominant Scots-Irish society and disappeared into the great American melting pot.

It is paradoxical that without knowing the origin of the label or its history many descendants want to embrace it now, without acknowledging the Jewish background, and without being Jewish themselves or having suffered the same experiences that gave the epithet its birth. Others, with ingrained anti-Semitism and utter complacency, instinctively deny both the letter and the spirit of the word.

Many thanks to Salomon & Victoria Cohen Professor in Spanish and Latin American Literature Ruth Fine, Chair of the Department of Romance and Latin American Studies, The Hebrew University, Jerusalem, for her help and suggestions with this essay.

ANCESTORS AND ENEMIES

Oh, they're all fled with thee,
Robin Adair!

3 SHALOM, Y'ALL

This little jeu d'esprit *was published in the* Appalachian Quarterly, *vol. 7, no. 2, pp. 80-89. Since that journal has gone out of existence (through no fault of ours, we hope), it is reprinted here.*

Recent investigations suggest the core gene pool of the mysterious Melungeon ethnic group that has long baffled Southern anthropologists is Sephardic Jewish. The Sephardim are one of the main divisions of Jewry. They are also known as Marranos or Ladino, Portuguese, Spanish, Hispanic, Iberian and Western Jews.

I had always suspected that my mother's family was Melungeon with some Indian blood. We proudly traced our heritage to Isaac Cooper of Grainger County, Tennessee and Wayne County, Kentucky, who married a daughter of the Cherokee chief Black Fox, or Enola (died 1811). My mother is a Cooper from Sand Mountain, a forlorn echo of the Appalachians in the tristate area of northeast Alabama. In fact, we were doubly descended from Black Fox, for another daughter married Chief William Davis (1753-1848), my grandmother Dovie Palestine Goble's ancestor. It was said that the Coopers were Irish and the Davises were — well, guesses ranged from Scottish to Australian. Both families came out of Daniel Boone's Kentucky and settled in the fastnesses of Sand Mountain when the Cherokee left on their forced removal in the 1830s. Family stories hinted that the Coopers started out as soldiers for the English Crown, won a baronetcy in Scotland from the earls of Shaftesbury, then served Oliver Cromwell until they had a falling out with him in Ireland.

Then I received a startling e-mail from Elizabeth Hirschman, a scholarly author and professor of marketing at Rutgers University in New Jersey. Titled simply "Cooper ethnicity," it detailed how we were distant cousins through the Coopers in Coeburn, Virginia, the Melungeon heartland. I agreed to read Hirschman's book-in-progress, *The Melungeons: The Last Lost Tribe in America.* All the surnames on my mother's side of the family were suddenly revealed to be Sephardic! What if I was Jewish-Indian? The thought conjured up images of peddlers in war bonnets selling tonics in a traveling medicine show.

Were there any historical Jewish Indian chiefs? I immediately asked the Internet search engine Jeeves, "Who is the most famous Jewish Indian?" The answer: Norman Greenbaum (60's musician and creator of the one-hit wonder "Spirit in the Sky"). That sent me on a bizarre journey through the obscurities of crypto-Judaism, Indian mascots, the theory of the Indians' descent from the lost tribes of Israel, Freemasonry, the Spanish Inquisition, the Watauga Settlements in Tennessee and the history of the Confederacy.

Jewish Indians, it seems, are an old joke. Bernard Malamud's posthumous novel *The People* is a classic instance of a shtick that can be traced to a "well-defined line of Jewish-American entertainment," in the words of one critic. It deals with a Jewish schlemiel who is adopted by the Indians out west and becomes Chief Jozip. The Austrian writer Else Lasker-Schueler styled herself an American Indian, and Franz Kafka joked that he wanted to be a "Red Indian." According to Lilian Friedberg, citing an article by Seth Wolitz, "the tradition of spoofing Jewish and Indian inter-relations...reaches back to a Yiddish playlet, *Tsvishn Indianer,*" an 1895 entertainment translated as "Among the Indians, or the Country Peddler." Fanny Brice's claim to fame was the song "I'm an Indian," and Eddie Cantor, Woody Allen and Mel Brooks milked the same gag. Today, Marx Toys makes an accessorized series of "Cherokee Chief Black Hair The Movable Indian," described as looking "very much like the actor Ed Ames (Mingo of the Daniel Boone show)," the Jewish-American entertainer.

But did the murky nether regions of American history contain any "real" Jewish Indians? The American Jewish Historical Society had one candidate that answered the description. Don Solomono Bibo, Jewish Indian Chief, was born in Prussia in 1853. His brothers, who settled in New

Mexico in 1866, preceded him west. The Bibo brothers worked for the Spiegelberg family of pioneer merchants. Eventually they set up a trading post to exchange goods with the Navajos, and Solomon joined them from Germany at the age of sixteen, in 1869. He soon became governor of the Acoma pueblo. In 1885, he married Juana Valle, the granddaughter of his predecessor, who converted to Judaism. Their children were sent to Hebrew school in San Francisco. "Solomon Bibo, governor of the Acomas, America's only known Jewish Indian chief, is buried with his Indian princess in the Jewish cemetery in Colma, California."

The New Mexico Jewish Historical Society dedicated its 12th annual conference in November 1999 to "the Jewish pioneers of the Territory of New Mexico and the Pueblo Indians with whom they became so close." The keynote speaker was Mel Marks, author of the groundbreaking 1995 book *Jews among the Indians.* A picture of Jake Gold, "among the first Jews to settle in Santa Fe, with unidentified Pueblo Indian woman and baby" decorated the program, and conference goers could view the first public display of Solomon Bibo's revolver.

The trail was becoming somewhat more credible and tantalizing. But how about Jews in the South? I learned from a brief article by Louis E. Schmier in the *Encyclopedia of Southern Culture* that Jews were more prominent in the civic affairs of the South than most people realize. Well appreciated are the facts that David Emanuel (1744-1810) was governor of Georgia (also the namesake for the county neighboring Bulloch County, where I now live), that some of the earliest Jewish communities were in Savannah, Charleston, Pensacola, St. Augustine, Baltimore, Natchez, Wheeling and Louisville, and that reform Judaism received its impetus largely from Southern Sephardic Jews. Perhaps not so well understood are where Southern Jews came from, why they settled in the places they did, and how they recognized and supported one another in various migrations through the Southland.

Some random points that are mentioned in the "Ethnic Life" section of the encyclopedia are:

"...[U]ntil the post-Civil War period, the centers of American Jewish life and the sources of many social, cultural, and religious institutional changes shaping the character of all American Jewry were found in Charleston and in Savannah, Ga., which had gathered a Jewish community as early as 1733."

"Individuals such as Mordecai Sheftall of Savannah and Francis Salvador of Charleston stood among the southern leadership during the American Revolution."

"...Jews such as Abraham Mordecai, who is credited with founding Montgomery, Ala., moved westward, occasionally joining other Jews who had been living along the Mississippi since the early 18th century."

"[Jews] started as peddlers and shopkeepers, and many rose to the ranks of the most prominent and influential businessmen...the Rich brothers in Georgia, the Sanger brothers as well as Neiman and Marcus in Texas, Godchaux in Louisiana, Psitz in Alabama, the Maas brothers in Florida, and the

Levine brothers in North Carolina."

"Adolph Ochs, who was from Chattanooga, developed the *New York Times* into the great American newspaper."

Brent Kennedy in *The Melungeons: The Resurrection of a Proud People* adds some intriguing sidelights, such as the Melungeon heritage of Abraham Lincoln and Jefferson Davis and the true ethnic mix of the Pamunkey/Powhatan Indians of Virginia. A final clue: the man on the Confederate $2 bill is Judah P. Benjamin (1811-1884), a Jew. What was going on here?

To continue in our quest let us consider the Indian trader James Adair and his *History of the American Indians* (London, 1775), one of the first encyclopedic works on Southeastern Indians. Largely dismissed as a misguided attempt to show Indians were descended from ancient Jews, the book is seldom read today. I can remember finding a rare copy of this curious volume in an antiquarian bookshop in Chicago, paying the hefty price tag and thinking, I now have the grail!

Who was James Adair? Until the year 2000, no one really knew. It may be instructive to quote the entire article dedicated to him in *The Dictionary of American Biography*:

ADAIR, James (c1709-1783), pioneer Indian trader, author, is said to have been born in County Antrim, Ireland. The dates given above are merely conjectural. The known facts of his life are few, gathered in the main from the personal incidents narrated in his book, The History of the American Indians (1775) and occasional references in South Carolina chronicles. A recent book, Adair History and Genealogy (1924), by J.B. Adair, gives many biographical details purporting to be based on family tradition, but few of them are verifiable by any available records. It is certain that Adair was highly educated. By 1735 he had come to America, probably entering at the port of Charleston, SC. In that year he engaged in trade with the Catawbas and Cherokees, continuing with them until 1744. He then established himself among the Chickasaws, whose villages were on the headwaters of the Yazoo, in Mississippi, where he remained for about six years. During the latter part of this period he frequently visited the Choctaws, in an effort to counteract the influence of the French and to win them to an alliance with the English. The effort was successful, but it involved him in difficulties with other traders and with James Glen, royal governor of South Carolina from 1743 to 1756, which resulted, he asserts, in his financial ruin. In 1751 he moved to District Ninety-six (the present Laurens County), SC, and resumed trade with the Cherokees, remaining there until about the end of 1759. His activities during these years covered a wide range. He was several times called in council by Gov. Glen, with whom he could never agree and whom he heartily detested. Among the Indians he was a diplomat and a peace maker, but he was also a fighter--"a valiant warrior," says Logan; and when he could not compose their quarrels he not infrequently took sides in their wars. At various times he was engaged in conflicts with the French. In the Indian war of 1760-61 he commanded a band of Chickasaws, receiving his supplies by way of

Mobile. In 1769 he visited New York City. Either then or a few years later he probably voyaged to London. Of his later life nothing authentic is recorded. He was, as the conclusion of his book amply shows, a vigorous defender of the rights of the colonies, but there appears to be no mention of him in Revolutionary annals. He is said to have been married and to have had several children and also to have died in North Carolina shortly after the close of the Revolution.

Adair is chiefly known through his history of the Indians. Primarily it is an argument that the Indians are the descendants of the ancient Jews. The theory was accepted by Elias Boudinot, one-time president of the Continental Congress, who gave it hearty support in his book, *A Star in the West* (1816) Adair's work has outlived its thesis. Its account of the various tribes, their manners, customs, their manners, and vocabularies, its depiction of scenes and its narration of incidents in his own eventful career, give it a permanent value. It is a record of close and intelligent observation, and its fidelity of fact has been generally acknowledged. The book must have required many years of toil. In his preface he says that it was written "among our old friendly Chickasaws" (doubtless during his second period of residence with them) and that the labor was attended by the greatest difficulties.

Though some passages may subsequently have been added, it was probably finished by the end of 1768. In the Georgia Gazette, of Savannah, October 11, 1769, appeared an item dated February 27th of that year, apparently copied from a New York newspaper, announcing the arrival of Adair in New York and saying that "he intends to print the Essays." The care with which the book is printed indicates that he gave it personal supervision through the press. From the dedication it is evident that he had the friendship of the noted Indian traders, Col. George Galphin and Col. George Croghan (with the former of whom he may for a time have been in partnership) and Sir William Johnson; and from various references it is certain that he was highly respected by those who knew him. Logan credits him with the quick penetration of the Indian audacity, cool self-possession, and great powers of endurance, and Volwiler says that he was one of the few men of ability who personally embarked in the Indian trade.

[J. H. Logan, A Hist. of the Upper Country of SC (1859); John Thos. Lee, letter in the Nation Aug 27, 1914; manuscript notes supplied by Robt. L. Meriwether; brief references in A.T. Volwriter, Geo. Croghan and the Westward Movement, 1741-1782 (1926) and Edward McCrady, Hist. of SC Under the Royal Government (1899).

Adair, then, was a cipher. New information surfaced only recently. Apparatchniks on the Internet brought to light a forgotten historical marker on Highway 710 near the town of Rowland in Robeson County, North Carolina. It noted that James Adair, Indian trader and historian, was buried nearby. Persistent delving turned up a lost will, preserved in an old genealogy compilation, *Kinfolks*, the labor of love of great-great-great-grandson William Curry Harllee. The will was filed in Elizabethtown, Bladen County (parent county of

Robeson), about 1778, probated apparently in 1787, and later destroyed in a courthouse fire. It names a wife, previously rumored to be Cheraw Indian, plus three daughters — no sons:

WILL OF JAMES ADAIR

In the name of God, "Amen." I, James Adair in Bladen County in North Carolina, being weak but praises be to the Almighty God, in perfect sense and memory, I do humbly make and ordain this my last Will and Testament in manner and form following:

I do recommend my soul to God who gave it hoping through the merits of my Lord and Blessed Savior Jesus Christ to obtain pardon of all my sins. My body I commit to the grave to be buried.

My Temporal Estate my just debts being paid I do humbly appoint my loving daughter Saranna McTyre my whole and sole Executor of this my last Will and Testament.

I give unto Robert Adair or his heirs near the town of Billymansborough and Nutrann a short mile of Gilgoram in the county of Antrim in Ireland ten pounds.

I give unto James Box or his heirs in the Island of Bennet the sum of nine pounds.

I give unto Alexander Johnston or his heirs in Ireland or his heirs in the county of Chester, Pennsylvania, the sum of seventeen pounds all proclamation money.

I give unto my daughter Saraanna McTyre, all my lands or improvements in Wilkinsons Swamp together with all my negroes and their increase to wit: Four negroes Pomp, Babby, Sam and Jack, two negro women named Hannah and Nelly, one negro girl named Lucy, my personal and real Estate both within and without doors, crop and stock together with all money, bonds, judgments, notes of hand, book accounts and debts whatsoever and whomsoever during her natural life and when my daughter Saraanna McTyre receives and collects in my money due on judgments, notes of hand and book debts, I desire it may be put out immediately on good security mortgages on improved lands and negroes until there is a fair and open trade from Guinea to this country for negro slaves, then to call in all the money into her hands immediately lay the money out in purchasing and buying negro slaves, boys and girls, and when bought then I give a part of the negroes so purchased and bought as has cost my executrix four hundred pounds proclamation money with their increase unto my daughter Elizabeth Hobson Cade during her life and at her death I give the said negroes with all their increase unto my three grandsons Stephen, James, and Washington Cade, and their heirs lawfully begotten forever, and the residue and remainder of the said purchase and bought negroes, after my daughter Cade has received her part and property as above mentioned then I give unto my daughter Susanna (sic) McTyer with all their increase during her life.

I give unto my grandson Adair McTyre the plantation whereon I now live one hundred acres more or less named Pached or Patcherly place on Wilkinson Swamp, together with all the improvements to him and his heirs lawfully begotten forever.

After my daughter Saranna McTyer's life I give

unto my Grandson one plow horse and one cow and calf two sow pigs and all the working tools within and without doors, suitable for carrying on a crop and corn and provision both without and within doors, should anything happen after my daughter's life. I give all my other lands more or less unto my grandson William McTyer and his heirs lawfully begotten forever when he comes of age.

I give unto my five grandchildren Adair, Elizabeth, Clark, Katrain, and William McTyer, all my negroes and their increase and my personal estate to be equally divided amongst them, to them and their heirs lawfully begotten forever after Saranna McTyre life.

I do give the free use of my means to my daughter Cades family as long as my daughter Saranna McTyre and Elizabeth Hobson Cade live convient [sic] one to another.

I give unto my daughter Agnes Gibson and to John Gibson one Shilling sterling.

I do desire my daughter Saranna McTyer take my daughter Agnes Gibson into her family should it so happen she is a widow and only one child and no good home, and maintain she and her child during widowhood and until her child comes of age, in meat drink lodging washing.

I do desire none of my estate may be sold by order of Court, when goods come as cheap as they have in the year 1774.

Then I do desire my Executrix will buy each of my daughters, Elizabeth Hobson Cade and Agnes Gibson a gown of Black Crepe and mourning ring.

In testimony of this my last Will and

Testament I hereunto set my hand and seal, this twenty first day of September one thousand seven hundred and seventy eight.

James Adair (seal)
Signed sealed and Witnessed
Archd McKissack
Benilla Bullard

(Source: Elizabethtown, Bladen Co., North Carolina, Record of Wills No. 1, p. 476, reprinted in "Kinfolks" by Wm. Harllee, pp. 1245-1247. –Thanks to Lisa Bowes of Old Saybrook, Conn. for this information.)

Robert Adair, remembered in the document with the not-insignificant bequest of 10 pounds, might be Sir Robert Adair (1763-1855), the son of Dr. Robin Adair and Lady Caroline Keppel. The popular ballad "Robin Adair" tells the story of an English lady who had a romantic adventure with a dashing and witty young man rejected by her family:

What's this dull town to me?
Robin's not near.
What was't I wished to see,
What wished to hear?
Where's all the joy and mirth
Made this town
A heav'n on earth?
Oh, they're all fled with thee,
Robin Adair!

Does history record any specifically Jewish traders among the Southeastern Indians? Benjamin Hawkins, the Indian agent, mentions one: "Abraham M. Mordecai, a Jew of bad character" (*Letters of Benjamin Hawkins 1796-1806*, page 168).

Pickens interviewed Mordecai for his history of early Alabama and wrote: "Abram Mordecai, an intelligent Jew, who dwelt fifty years in the Creek Nation, confidently believed that the Indians were originally of his people." Where there are open Jews is it not reasonable to expect there were also undeclared Jews? Many Indian traders in the Southeast not labeled as such appear to have Sephardic names: Benjamin and James Burges (from the Spanish city of Burgos?—they later changed the name to Burkes and were intermarried with the Coopers), William and Joseph Cooper (a trail guide and linguister active among the Cherokee since 1710, said to be the first ones), Cornelius Dougherty (since 1724—another family that moved from the Lower Towns to the Upper Towns in Tennessee), Eleazor Wiggans (whose Indian name was Old Rabbit, license revoked 1714, a corroborator of the Jewish descent theory about Indians), James Beamer (from Boehmer, "Bohemian"?), the namesake of the Cherokee headman called Judd's ("Jew's") Friend, John and Daniel Ross, Christian Russel ("a Silician"), Nicolas White ("a native of Mersailles, but resident in this nation 30 years"), Mrs. Durant (a female trader), Obediah Low, John Van, James Lessle (Lesley), James Lewis, Aron Harad, Zachariah Cox (a land developer), Richard Sparks (a captain at Tellico Blockhouse), Gen. James Robertson (founder of Nashville, Roberson, "of Moro District"), Abraham Gindrat, Davis (a blacksmith), John Marino ("a Spaniard"), John Sheppard, John Clark, McBean, and McKee. Moreover, the trading houses of Clark in Virginia; Rae, Galphin and McGillivray of

Augusta; Panton, Leslie, and Company in Pensacola and the Francis family of silversmiths appear to have Sephardic mercantile connections in London, Amsterdam, Barbados and the Barbary Coast.

Most traders not of the itinerant or "fly-by-night" kind married a daughter or niece of the relevant Cherokee, Choctaw, Chickasaw or Creek headman. It was a common prerequisite for anyone remaining within the nation over one winter to take a wife and become an adoptive citizen. Sequoyah's father Nathaniel Gist followed this practice, marrying Wurteh, or Wutteh, said to be a chief's daughter. He subsequently abandoned her and went back to his white wife in Kentucky. Beloved woman Nancy Ward's husband Bryant Ward followed the same pattern of behavior. The mixed breed Hildis Harjo, better known as Josiah Francis, was a typical product of such unions. Another such in my family history was Dr. William Alexander Davis (born about 1790), the son of the previously mentioned William Davis and Mary Ann Black. He signed the treaty of July 8, 1817 as Young Davis, between Charles Hicks and Saunooka. By the time of the Treaty of New Echota in 1835 he was recognized as a chief. He married Mary Burns, the daughter of Chief Arthur (or Author) Burns and Aky Lowrey, daughter of Chief George Lowrey. With the chiefdom, he inherited the North Sauty reservation near Blowing Cave on Sand Mountain, comprising 640 acres. He sold this just before the Cherokee removal.

A doctor and a lawyer? That seems like every Jewish mother's dream. Dutifully, I input the new information, but my genealogy program gave me a firm error message. Too many titles. It reminded me of an old Viennese joke. Count Rudi goes on vacation and sends Count Bobi a postcard. When they meet again in the city, Count Bobi asks why there was no message included on the card. Count Rudi explains that after he wrote in all of Count Bobi's titles—two doctorates, an honorary professorship, and a rank of petty nobility conferred on his family by the Kaiser—there was no room left for any greetings.

Could the trader James Adair's name have been Robin (Reuben)? Several genealogies have it so. According to family tradition, it was a pet name. We have no picture of James Adair, only family recollections of him as "splendidly muscular, fine-looking, broad-shouldered, bearded man of a little more than medium height." But his nephew John Adair became governor of Kentucky and favored posterity with a likeness (Illustration 3). Could Adair, the honorary chief of the Chickasaws and first white man to see the Cumberland Gap, actually have been an Irish, or Scottish, Jew? Once again we seem to have landed in the realm of entertainment. Such a supposition, however, would go far to explain how a frontier adventurer who traveled light, was able to fill his book with Hebrew words and phrases, compiling it in a Chickasaw lodge in the Mississippi wilderness at a time when only a handful of Christians, mostly Oxford and Sorbonne divines, knew Hebrew. Adam Smith lamented in *The Wealth of Nations*, published the same year as Adair's *History,* that there was little or no reason to even study Hebrew.

Upstanding Jews learned how to read and write it, particularly Sephardic Jews rediscovering their heritage in Enlightenment England and Holland. Adair even slips on at least one occasion and speaks of Hebrew greeting customs as "*our* method of salutation" (p. 47). He also quotes current Hebrew witticisms and notes that the Hebrew heard today is more guttural than the dialect of the American Indians.

Notice the harsh treatment Adair accords his daughter Agnes, leaving her and her husband John Gibson the nominal sum of only one shilling (if he had left her nothing, she could have protested to the probate court that he simply forgot her). John was one of the "mulatto" Gibsons of the Great Pee Dee river valley region. Gideon Gibson stands large on the pages of history for his role in the so-called Regulators Revolt. The Gideon Glass Antiques Store today pays testimony to the "richest man in South Carolina" of his time. When members of the Gibson family first moved to the state in 1731, representatives in the House of Assembly complained "several free colored men with their white wives had immigrated from Virginia." Governor Robert Johnson summoned Gibson and his family and reported:

I have had them before me in Council and upon Examination find that they are not Negroes nor Slaves but Free people, That the Father of them here is named Gideon Gibson and his Father was also free, I have been informed by a person who has lived in Virginia that this Gibson has lived there Several Years in good Repute and by his papers that he has produced before me that his transactions there have been very regular. That he has for several years paid Taxes for two tracts of Land and had several Negroes of his own, That he is a Carpenter by Trade and is come hither for the support of his Family [Box 2, bundle: S.C. Minutes of House of Burgesses (1730-35), 9, Parish Transcripts, N.Y. Hist. Soc. By Jordan, *White over Black,* 172.]

The Gibsons are discussed as Melungeons in Brent Kennedy and as true-to-form Sephardic Jews in Hirschman. Melungeon Gibsons derive their origins from the Chavis family, one of the oldest Portuguese-Jewish names in America. If they are Jewish, it is ironic—and probably funnier than any Fanny Brice skit—that historians trot them forth as shining examples of non-slave African American colonials owning land and marrying white women.

The early years of the nineteenth century were a time when the forces of westward expansion in the new American Republic violently collided with the lives of the Cherokee. These ancient mountaineers of the South have passed into modern history as the most numerous and probably the most adaptable of all Indians. Illustration 4 depicts Moses Looney, a half-brother of Cherokee Chief John Looney, the son of Captain John Looney and the sister of Black Fox. Chief Looney fought with Andrew Jackson at Horse Shoe Bend, signed the act of union between the Eastern and Western Cherokee (with his cousin Sequoyah) and died on May 15, 1846 in Washington, D.C., while acting as a delegate for the Indians. Less is known about Moses. He married a cousin, Mary Guest, a descendant of the Baltimore Indian trader and spy, Christopher Gist, Sequoyah's white grandfather. (Curiously, a remote ancestor had married Edith Cromwell, a relative of the Lord Protector.) This rare early photograph shows him in the final decade of his life (he died January 9, 1855). He is wearing a "Cherokee" turban similar to that worn by Sequoyah and Chief George Lowrey.

The first Looney entered the port of Philadelphia in 1731 and like many new arrivals joined the Quakers. The Luna clan (note the spelling, hardly an English-sounding name and more likely Spanish or Portuguese) then became one of seventy families that moved south to the colony of Virginia with Alexander Ross and Morgan Bryan, settling in Orange County (now Frederick) and moving to Augusta, then Botetourt, where the patriarch of the family, Robert Looney, died September 14, 1769. The Looney men distinguished themselves by building and operating ferries and forts, fighting at Kings Mountain and later against the Cherokee. When the State of Franklin was daringly proposed Looneys were in the thick of it, and when James Robertson established the Cumberland settlement in Nashville many of them followed westward. Moses Looney's stomping ground was Maury County. His father and brothers moved from Maury to St. Clair County, Alabama after the Creek War. Looney branches later went to Texas with Stephen Austin and Sam Houston. At least one kept going to Old Mexico. Today near the town of Celaya in Guanajuato province lives a band of blond haired, blue-eyed Cherokees who have reverted to the original name and call themselves Luna. The inventor of the Cherokee system of writing, Sequoyah, arguably the most famous Southern Indian chief, is said to be buried about twelve miles out of town (information of Molly Running Wolf Mills, a Sequoyah descendant in St. Thomas, Virgin Islands).

In the 1820s the Looneys were among the first pioneer white families in the area of Alabama now home to the glorious Bankhead National Forest. The second-largest wilderness area east of the Mississippi, it stretches almost completely across the state, from Fox's Mountain, Creekpath on Sand Mountain and Deerhead Cove in the east to Choctaw and Chickasaw country in the west. A mute reminder of the Indian gift to the pioneers is the Looney Tavern, previously known as the Black Fox Tavern, near Cullman. The two-story double-dogtrot log cabin recently acquired an amphitheatre complex, complete with steamboat cruises and putt-putt golf. An outdoor pageant "The Incident at Looney Tavern" attracts tourists from all over. Few, however, probably know the complete saga of the Looneys. Once again, history seems to have dissolved into entertainment....

Genealogy is—or should be—a window on history. Before discovering the "key," I never could fathom why my Coopers lived where they lived, married whom they married and gave their children monikers like Mahala, Harmon, Zachariah, Palestine, Elzina, Mariah, Huston, Delitha, Malilah, Millea, Alvis, Milton, Elvirah, Manorah, Lila, Lula, Lillie, Feny, Selena, Sophia, Telitha and (my favorite) Lucinderella. Though some of these are Biblical, they are not the names of

Christian saints. How to explain that my 3rd-great grandfather Isaac Cooper, pet-name Zack, married Mahala Jane Blevins, pet-name Linny, and they went all over the South as railroaders? Coopers exchanged letters with family members in Arkansas, Texas and Mississippi at a time when the literacy rate was, in general, very low. They bought land with cash on the barrelhead and borrowed money from informal banks owned by extended kin (the Lowreys helped the Coopers and others with loans in the Great Depression). They remained to found towns like Guntersville, Adairsville, Willstown and Cooperstown after the Indians were removed. They spoke the Cherokee, Chickasaw and Choctaw languages and knew arcane arts like joining, engraving, silversmithing and smelting. Many, like my grandfather Dolphus Cooper (1881-1960), had jet-black hair, olive complexions and deep blue eyes.

Isaac Cooper, described as Choctaw-Cherokee-Scotch-Irish, was the son of Nancy Black Fox, a Cherokee chief's daughter. He was born in an ambiguous place on the Kentucky-Tennessee line claimed by both states, at one time part of Virginia, North Carolina, and the lost states of Franklin and Transylvania. His father Isaac disappeared into another sort of Bermuda Triangle where Virginia, Pennsylvania, and Ohio come together, and is remembered today in the records of the Wheeling (W. Va.) Temple Shalom congregation. The younger Isaac worked for the Little South Fork Salt and Iron Works, participated in the accidental sinking of the world's first oil well and went off to conquer Mexico with Gen. Winfield Scott after building a farmstead for his large family in Deerhead Cove (Anawaika), another place "not on the map." (Tucked away under the brow of Fox Mountain behind a maze of dirt roads, it is nigh unto impossible to find even today.) He is buried in Mexico in the Church of San Francisco, built 1775, near the Plaza de la Reforma, once part of a Franciscan convent, used as a hospital by the American army during the 1847-1848 occupation of Vera Cruz. These were no storybook Indians. Nor were they ordinary Jews. Their lives were the stuff of legend, and of some strange ethnic mix.

I excitedly called my 84-year-old mother in Florida. "Mother, I found out what the Coopers were, or are — they're, uh, Jewish!" Long silence on the other end. "Mother, you yourself are, uh, Jewish!" More silence, then finally, "Well, what of it?" I was glad she did not go into denial.

Which reminds me…how many Jewish Indians does it take to change a light bulb?

Light bulb? What light bulb?

ANCESTORS AND ENEMIES

Gomez with the Indians

4 YOU WILL NEVER FIND OUT THE TRUTH

A human life is like a single letter in the alphabet. It can be meaningless, or it can be part of a great meaning. — Jewish Theological Seminary of America

"You will never find out the truth about my mother's people," sneered Elzina when we met with her in her Victorian cottage in Huntsville. Elzina was Teresa's aunt, my father-in-law's older sister. Teresa and I had both recently discovered we were Melungeon—or at least of Melungeon descent. Teresa wondered especially about the Rameys, Elzina's mother's people. So we went to see this formidable maiden aunt, keeper of skeletons and reigning matriarch of the family. From her childhood Teresa remembered her as tightlipped, scowling, always garbed in black satin dresses and lace-up boots. Elzina LaVera Grimwood was a schoolteacher, daughter and granddaughter of schoolteachers, sixth in a series of Tennessee Elzinas that stretched back to the days of Daniel Boone. As we drove away through the mountains, Teresa remarked that her aunt would not have used those words if the big mystery was that the Ramey family had Indian blood, or came from France. "Maybe they were bootleggers," I suggested. "Or Gypsies." Speculate as we may it was hard to guess what dreadful stigma lay concealed in the family genealogy. Elzina carried the secret to her grave.

As Elzina lay on her deathbed, I received an email from Melungeon researcher Elizabeth Hirschman. It suggested that my Cooper family was of Sephardic Jewish derivation. I knew immediately Beth was right. The simple truth was that Melungeons, witness the Coopers and Rameys, were crypto-Jews.

But how could we be Jewish and Indian at once?

When the indigenous people of the Americas began to be identified as possible descendants of the lost tribes of the Hebrews by the English, Menasseh ben Israel, chief rabbi of Amsterdam, petitioned Cromwell to readmit Jews into England (The Hope of Israel, 1648). In actuality, the book he wrote was more a public relations gesture than work of dispassionate scholarship. Marrano lobbyists took up the issue and played to the Puritan party in parliament. The Puritans believed they were in line to receive the coveted crown of a New Millennium that according to prophecy would be bestowed on the Christian sect able to unite all peoples of the realm, including the Jews and Indians, in one faith.

The synagogue to which my wife and I belong in Savannah, the third oldest in America, is named after Ben Israel's influential book—Mickve Israel. This book was celebrated by Jews because it contained the first modern manifesto of rights, addressed to Oliver Cromwell, whose family had been Jewish in prior times. While no act of reentry ended up being accepted or formally passed into law, Jews began to trickle into England as foreigners with limited rights. Throughout the Georgian period they exerted a strong influence on trade, monetary policy and foreign affairs, albeit keeping behind the scenes. They maintained a foothold in both Whig and Tory camps and made the most of a feeling of kinship sensed by many British aristocratic families. One such aristocrat was Anthony Ashley-Cooper, 1st earl of Shaftesbury and a Lord Proprietor of the English colonies. Lord Ashley was a secret Mason, freethinker and suspected crypto-Jew. It was his secretary John Locke, who drafted the famous "The Fundamental Constitutions of Carolina." This was the first governmental charter to specifically include Jews by name in an edict of religious tolerance. Subsequently, Charleston became the most populous Jewish community. Shaftesbury fell from grace, he strongly opposed James's marriage with the Spanish enfanta, and he died in exile in Amsterdam. But a religious congregation began to form in London about this same time led by the very Spanish-Portuguese Jewish merchants Lord

Ashley threw his lot in with. They discretely called themselves, in Portuguese, "People of The Nation," not trumpeting forth what nation that might be. At a time when England was virulently anti-Catholic, they had the privilege of maintaining their own Catholic chapel and confessional in London.

Sephardic rabbis in New York and Newport during this era issued responsa (juridical opinions) enjoining Jews not to mistreat Indians, considering they might be descendants of the Ten Lost Tribes of Israel. American and Caribbean Jewish law condoned marriage between Jews and Indians. The progeny of such unions were ruled to be Jewish.

My mother frequently mentioned that our family was a "duke's mixture." What did that even mean?

The symbol of the London Sephardic presence has always been Bevis Marks Synagogue. Founded in 1703, Bevis Marks just celebrated its 300th anniversary. Prince Charles was the guest of honor. Charles said on the occasion that he had never noticed the understated architectural masterpiece of Bevis Marks in East London before. That was because it was built on a side street in the Financial District, facing in so as not to attract notice or give offense. By settled policy, even the monuments of crypto-Jews are unobtrusive. Appropriately, East London is the origin of the expression "duke's mixture." Dukes Fields outside London's medieval walls traditionally has been home to teeming multitudes of poor immigrants of every nationality. It was there that the Ashkenazi Great Synagogue rose.

In British ports of call such as Barbados,

Jamaica, New York, Newport, Charleston and St. Eustachius, Jews could become citizens of the land in a legal process called denizening. They could vote, serve in the armed forces and hold office. For Jews, this opened the door to an extraordinary series of efforts to migrate to the New World and build communities for themselves. Merchants, hatters, carpenters, ironworkers—they arrived in the ports of Philadelphia, Baltimore, Charleston and Savannah and quietly put down roots. Many later blended with the Indian nations in the interior. In some cases—among the Lumbees, Pamunkey and Cherokee—-Sephardim intermarried and took over the machinery of trade relations and government. Jewish Cherokee chiefs such as Will Webber, John Ross, George Guess, John Looney, George Lowrey and Sam Houston signed treaties, wrote laws and constitutions and led their people westward to Arkansas, Oklahoma and Texas.

Luis Moses Gomez, a Portuguese Jew fleeing from the Spanish Inquisition, came to New England, made a pact with the Mohican Indians and built Gomez Mill House in Newburgh, N.Y at the intersection of six Indian paths. The castlelike dwelling is the oldest surviving Jewish residence in North America. Gomez was also the first parnas (president) of Sheareth Israel, New York's oldest synagogue. The subsequent story of these "big city" Jews is told in Stephen Birmingham's delightful book The Grandees. They financed and fed George Washington's army, won the War of Independence, gave the world Saks 5th Avenue, saw to it that the Saxe-Coburg became Europe's most successful ruling dynasty, built the Waldorf-Astoria and established Barnard College along with a host of other institutions.

Histories of American Jewry are often biased toward Ashkenazi Jews. Jacob Rader Marcus' series, The Colonial American Jew (3 vols.), is typical and paradigmatic. Most books followed his lead and focused on prominent individuals, giving pride of place to East Coast congregations. The story of American Jews is "New York-centric." Little work has been done to tell the story of the Sephardic diaspora in an American context. Jews in the South, the Ohio valley and along the Mississippi receive short shrift. Because of this lopsided treatment, estimates of the total number of Jews in early America are far too conservative. Marcus stated in the 1930s that at the time of the American Revolution there were no more than 2,000 Jews, concentrated in about ten coastal cities. Lancaster, Pennsylvania was the only inland community included in the survey. It is hard to reconcile this absurdly low number with the more than 50,000 Jewish Confederate soldiers who fought in the War Between the States seventy-five years later. We know about them because they refused to eat pork in their rations, requested the Sabbath off for religious purposes and were buried with Hebrew rites. They are all in the records, many of them bearing what we now regard as "Melungeon" surnames.

Marcus was also responsible for the sleight-of-hand of ignoring Jewish-sounding names and refusing to consider Jewish converts as Jews. Crypto-Jews were not Jews in his mind. Half a century later, however, if a family bears the name Cohen, Cone or Jacobs it is regarded as Jewish, at least by origin and ancestry, while Jewish converts to Christianity may be counted as "lapsed" Jews, but Jews nonetheless.

Certain states like North Carolina and Maryland are very poorly served in standard Jewish histories. If anyone doubts that early American Jewish demographics are in need of revision, consider the case of Sampson County, N.C. The 1790 Federal census had a 4th column between the number of females and slaves in the household that enumerated "Other Free Persons." It was up to the census taker how to interpret this. In Sampson County, just upland from Wilmington, he seems to have used this category for Jews and Indians. C.D. Brewington, "a distinguished native of Sampson Co.," wrote The Five Civilized Indian Tribes of Eastern North Carolina with "historical facts about these Indians whose descendants are still here" and "evidence of their intermarriage and life with the Whites from Sir Walter Raleigh's Lost Colony." Many identified as Coharie Indians, later as Lumbee. Apparently Brewington's ancestors are listed as "Other" in the household of Ann Brewington, where there are 3 "other" and nobody else. We suspect entries that are only first names like Hannah without a surname also indicated Indians, specifically Indians living in the settlements, not in an Indian community, thus probably Jewish Indians ("Old Natt"). Here are some more "other" households:

Joseph Williams 4
Hannah Williams

Nathaniel Revil 13
Jack Waldon
Crecy Williams
Old Natt 2
Molly Clewis 3
Rachael Green
Cloeraly 4
Mary Wiggins 6
Levi Emmanuel 5
Becky Cobb 3
David Terry 4
Ephraim Emmanuel
John Flowers
Davis
Isabella Jones, w/ 2 slaves
Boon
Samuel Bell (Bladen)
Many Joneses
Barfoot
Jacob(s) 39 altogether
Pages
Burnet
Johnston
Perry, Chas. & Collop, 15
Demery
Cumbo (Onslow)
James Sweet
Green
Freeman
Williams
Grice (may be Grimes)
Hannah, with 1 slave
Catherine Wren
Powell

Hesse, with 3 slaves
Cavers (Chavis)
Sanders (<Alexander)
Jemboy, with 6 slaves
Aithcock
Scott
Abraham Jacobs 3
John Emmanuel
Jack Mainor
(John Cooper, white)
Jesse Emmanuel
Nicholas Emmanuel 5
Moses Carter 9
Henry Carter 8
Patty Wiggins 5
Neighboring counties Duplin, Bladen, Brunswick, Johnson, Onslow and New Hanover have some, but not as many, "others."
Davis
Isabella Jones, w/ 2 slaves
Boon
Samuel Bell (Bladen)
Many Joneses
Barfoot
Jacob(s) 39 altogether
Pages
Burnet
Johnston
Perry, Chas. & Collop, 15
Demery
Cumbo (Onslow)
James Sweet
Green
Freeman

Williams
Grice (may be Grimes)
Hannah, with 1 slave
Catherine Wren
Powell
Hesse, with 3 slaves
Cavers (Chavis)
Sanders (<Alexander)
Jemboy, with 6 slaves
Aithcock
Scott

A Will West was in Bladen—perhaps my wife's Wests, who became Lumbee in Robeson. Minor becomes a common Melungeon name, as does Williams, Green, Perry, Davis, Bell, Chavis, and Cumbo. John Flowers may have begun life as Johann Blum, or John Bloom. The Jewish hero of James Joyce's Ulysses was Leopold Bloom of Dublin Town. Waldon is probably the same as Wallen, one of the early explorer families of Tennessee, the namesake for Waldens Ridge. Wiggins is probably related to Eleazar Wiggans, a prominent Jewish trader among the Yuchi and other Indians. Nearly every first name and surname is Hebrew and Jewish. A Jew named Emmanuel later became governor of Georgia. John, Fleet, Core, William and Daniel Cooper were in Sampson at the time (one of my lines, known to be crypto-Jewish, like Boone). Also, there is a former town on the South River named Lisbon! Some of these, if not the majority, were evidently Portuguese Jews, and it is likely that many persons counted as "taxed Indians" were actually Jewish Indians or just plain Jews.

Before the time of the Revolution, there was a rabbi, shul and Hebrew library in the little town of Warrenton in Bute County on the North Carolina Piedmont. The parnassim of the congregation used a Freemason's Lodge as their cover. My 6th-great-grandfather William Cooper, who accompanied Daniel Boone to Kentucky and planted the first corn crop there, was a member.

The earliest depositions of Lumbee Indians, not taken until the late nineteenth century, make it clear that an important portion of their founding families came to the swamplands of Robeson County from northeast North Carolina, just inland from the Lost Colony. Now Lumbee is an invented name, a back formation based on the place-names Lumberton and Lumber River. The oldest name is Lumberton, which I believe was originally Lombard-town, though I have no way of proving this. The reason? The jewelry and financial districts in metropolises like London and Philadelphia were invariably named Lombard Street. That is where "Lombard law" or mercantile law prevailed. "Lombard" and "Jewish merchant" were often synonymous. In medieval Oxford, Lombard-Hall was named after its Jewish proprietor (Anglia Judaica, by D'Blossiers Tovey). The oldest British Jews were Lombards and other Italians; they were joined by French-speaking Jews brought over by William the Conqueror. Thus we find a great deal of overlap between Lumbee and Melungeon names. The common denominator is Jewish. The original appeal of these swamps straddling the North and South Carolina state line lay in their rich, secret pig iron and coal beds. We find in the will of Israel Roberson preserved in the Wrightsboro Quaker records in 1773 an exact description of one of them ("...One hundred acres of land Lying on the head of the Beaver Dam in South Carolina where it is thought there is a Iron Mine").

Glassmaking, a Jewish monopoly through the ages, was also practiced there. The Gibsons of South Carolina with their glassworks and showrooms became that state's first millionaires. Robeson County was later named for a Robertson—the same family that founded Watauga and Nashville. The attractiveness to Jews and crypto-Jews of all these locales was as a safe haven where central authority did not exert itself very strongly. This explains how several Indian groups—Tuscarora, Coharie, Catawba, Saponi, Croatan, Ocaneechi, Cheraw (Juda, literally "Jewish Indians" in contemporary Spanish accounts), Tudelo and so forth—came together to form the Lumbees. No Indian languages were ever spoken by tribal members in modern times. The Lumbee today consequently have a difficult case to make to the U.S. Federal Government to become recognized.

An example of a common Lumbee name derivable from a medieval Jewish Lombard family is Braveboy. A 1292 census of Paris lists numerous wealthy Jews from Brabant, a Flemish city with ties to the cloth, weaving and woolen industry of Lombardy (de Brabant, Brébois). Bradby, a family name that supplied multiple chiefs to the Pamunkey Indians of Virginia, is probably a corruption of Brebois as well.

Covers for Judaic communities ranged from the Huguenots, Quakers, Freemasonry, Ulster Presbyterianism and Primitive Baptist churches to even Catholicism, which may have been the perfect disguise, especially in Maryland. Persons having Semitic looks explained their dark features by saying they were Black Dutch, Black Irish, Black Douglas, Black MacDonald and so forth. The War of Jenkins Ear and return of Florida to Spain in the 1780s, with the prospects of the Inquisition expanding its activities in English territories, produced a panic and brought an inrush of colonists to Tennessee. Because of numerous factors Tennessee has always acted as a magnet for Jews. John Adair, for instance, arrived with his family in Baltimore in 1753 and made a beeline for the Holston River. He later lent his storehouse to provision the Cumberland settlers under James Robertson. With the failure of the State of Franklin and such developments as the Yazoo Land Fraud, hopes for a true Jewish homeland soon focused on Missouri, Arkansas, Texas and farther west. Only when Spain dropped out as a player north of Mexico, and the Spanish Inquisition faded away as a real menace, did Jews in America as also in Britain feel they could return to the open practice of Judaism, if they still desired it. Usually this occurred without benefit of a haham, rabbi, Hebrew school or synagogue. They regarded America as their permanent new homes now and had little yearning for their former ones, while Zionistic dreams of living in Israel were far in the future. Their weakness in religious instruction and lack of connections with religious centers prevented them from producing spiritual leaders of their own. The first synagogues west of the Alleghenies were in places like Frankfort and Wheeling.

A final gasp of crypto-Jewish behavior can be traced in the careers of outlaws Frank and Jesse James (originally Hyam), the "last Cherokee warrior" Zeke Proctor and Lumbee folk hero Henry Berry Lowrie. According to Elizabeth Hirschman, who researched Jesse James's genealogy, not only was James a Melungeon but he was "line-bred." Most people in his family for several generations, including Jesse himself, married first cousins. Surnames were Cole, Poor, Mims, Hines, Thomason, Woodson, and Gardener. Reconstruction, the nativist movement and rise of the Ku Klux Klan destroyed a proud legacy and left the Melungeons a mystery even to themselves.

It cannot be our purpose here to follow the westward developments that produced Watauga, Nashville and the other experiments in pioneer government, culminating ultimately with the Republic of Texas. All these events produced splinter movements after the tide of settlement moved on. Pockets of people were left behind that are today known or suspected to be or reminiscent of Melungeons. The nucleus of early crypto-Jews in East Tennessee and surrounding areas continued to identify and stand out as Melungeon. But there were other Melungeon communities with varying numbers of people in them, as shown in the following census taken from an article by Bette Sue McElroy in Northeast Alabama Settlers, volume 22 (October 1983):

ANCESTORS AND ENEMIES

Melungeon Communities in 1950

Jackson Co., Ala.	70
Clay Co., Ky.	460
Floyd Co., Ky.	1680
Jackson Co., Ky.	140
Johnson Co., Ky.	420
Knott Co., Ky.	2420
Letcher Co., Ky.	1920
Magofin Co., Ky.	670
Whitney Co., Ky.	180

My father-in-law Dr. F. M. Grimwood of Pensacola was Elzina's younger brother and grew up like her in rural north Alabama near the Tennessee line. When my wife and I confronted him, he ticked off several items that qualify as Jewish customs, including throwing a silver coin into a baby boy's first bath water. He also pulled out a picture of himself at an early age wearing a kippah (small cap for prayer). The church his parents sent him to was an austere Pentecostal denomination known as Camelite, Carmelite or Campbellite. He remembered that an aunt "sang in the Jewish temple." Otherwise, he was raised with

89

no knowledge of a Jewish background.

If there were crypto-Jews on the frontier, why did they leave no monuments such as temples and cemeteries? We believe they certainly did. We know of one outstanding candidate, a stone temple built in 1756 in the Shenandoah Valley. Whether it still stands, I cannot say, but its endowment was commemorated in a slab seven feet long placed over the grave of John McKee in Timber Ridge Cemetery, near Lexington, Va. John McKee was born 1703 in Glasgow and died 1773 in Virginia. According to the inscription, he made his way to Ireland and thence to America, arriving in the Valley of Virginia by the time he was 33 or 34. He "brought with him the spirit of religious liberty, as his main object seems to have been to colonize and build a house of worship." One may wonder why, if it was Presbyterianism he wished to practice, he did not remain in Scotland or northern Ireland, where that denomination was the official religion. Davidsons, Porters (a self-confessed Portuguese family from Saponi territory about Fort Christanna), McCorkles, Coopers, Houstons, Baileys, Kennedys, McClungs and Alexanders were fellow members of this community. Gen. Sam Houston's father donated the land for the "church." As for the Alexanders, they were earls of Stirling, having arrived in Scotland around 1500, and having quickly become allied with the Forbes (Feibush, Phoebus) family. One branch immigrated to Maryland, where many of them are buried in Jewish-owned cemeteries. Other members of the clan went to Charleston and Savannah and joined the Masons and Sephardic Jewish upper crust in those cities (Malcolm H. Stern, Americans of Jewish Descent. A Compendium of Genealogy).

Alexanders were also involved in the extremely lucrative Caribbean-Mediterranean triangular trade of Panton, Leslie & Co., headquartered in Spanish Pensacola. As Scotsmen and Protestants in one guise and Jews or Spaniards in another, they received the freedom of the port in Havana as well as Glasgow, Amsterdam, Cadiz, Gibraltar and the Barbary Coast.

I believe there was a practicing Jewish-Indian-Melungeon hazzan (Jewish community functionary) in Wayne County, Kentucky, active from the 1790s until the time of Indian removal. My fourth great-grandfather Isaac Cooper was a Sephardic-Jewish-Choctaw born about 1775 in Rowan County, North Carolina. His grandfather William Cooper acted as Daniel Boone's scout and planted the first corn crop in Kentucky. Isaac fought in the Indian Wars and married Nancy Black Fox about 1795 in Tennessee. Nancy was daughter of Chief Black Fox and Attakullakulla's daughter, sometimes called Melba. Cooper was a soldier and also a gunsmith, ordinance expert and ironworker. He is named in the List of Taxes and Taxable Property in the Bounds of Capt. (William) Bean's Company, returned by William Stone, Esquire, in 1799. This locale lay in Cherokee country along the Holston River and Clinch Mountain in Tennessee, later Grainger County (Watauga Country, or State of Franklin). William Bean Sr.'s was the first white cabin in those parts, and it stood in the center of an apparently older Melungeon settlement. Here the "overmountain men" met at Sycamore Shoals to muster for the Battle of Kings Mountain. Beans Station on Clinch Mountain was later a notable inn and fort, the largest stagehouse between New Orleans and Washington City. Cooper acquired his property from Elizabeth Bean and Robert Blair. Elizabeth Bean was the widow of William Bean, Jr. who died in Grainger County in 1798. Her maiden name was Blair; she remarried to a Shaw. Capt. William Bean was a son of the famous Mrs. Lydia Russell Bean whose life was saved by Nancy Ward, the Cherokee Beloved Woman. He married Elizabeth Blair in Tennessee in 1782. A Bean-Blair-Cooper deed from these years shows land transactions were all within the family.

Through her connection with the Beans, Nancy Ward introduced the first cattle, swine, dairy products and looms into the Cherokee Nation.

In 1807, John Francis, another Indian fighter-turned-trader, first reported the discovery of saltwater along the Big South Fork of the Cumberland River. The initial discovery was reported to be "near the mouth of Bear Creek, where Richard Slavey now lives." Francis and Slavey petitioned the State Legislature and in 1811 received a Grant for 1000 acres, conditional upon their production of 1000 bushels of salt. Francis received another grant just south of the 1000-acre tract for the same purpose. Marcus Huling, working with Col. James Stone, sank another saltwater well, on the site of Francis's other grant. Stephen F. Conn, Martin Beaty and a host of others, including Isaac Cooper, became involved in these enterprises in several different ways. This activity started a series of lawsuits lasting up into the 1830s and caused the accidental sinking of the world's first oil well. The Francises were also intermarried with the Coopers, as were Troxells, Carters, Denneys, Blevinses, Burkes, Farrises, McCorkles, Gregorys, Adairs, Wallace/Lovelaces and Nichols/Nicholases. All these families, moreover, were linked with the Cherokee-Chickasaw-Choctaw-Powhatan ascendant hierarchies of the time. A common denominator in all these families was their Judaism. Isaac Cooper appears to have acted as a general religious factotum for life-change events, marrying young people, even visiting Jews from New York City in 1797, serving as character witness for residents in local courts, and possibly performing circumcisions and funerals. He was, in effect, a hazzan.

If doubts should be expressed whether the Coopers were openly Jewish or only secretly so, or long washed of their Jewishness, I have a copy of letters written in 1848 between two of Isaac Cooper's sons-in-law, John Adair and John Lovelace, husbands respectively of Sarah Cooper and Mary Cooper. One calls the other, affectionately, a "Jew." These families were not only literate but had storekeeping and accounting skills, something rare on the frontier.

People have often remarked upon the polyglot character of common Melungeon surnames. There appears to be no consistency to them. Scottish, Irish, Welsh, German, English, French, and Spanish/Portuguese mix together willy-nilly, and a family of one bent will marry with another apparently without rhyme or reason. Once the

Jewish identity underlying Melungeons is realized, everything falls into place.

In conclusion, we have looked at a number of pre-Revolutionary Tennessee families who were Melungeon and Jewish—more precisely, crypto-Jewish. All intermarried for religious motives, effectively keeping their secrets within the family. In some cases, for instance the Gists, Rameys, Alexanders and Coopers, we have contemporary records and evidence specifically naming them as Jews. I have argued that Judaism was the bond that brought them together on the frontier. It is of no importance that many of their descendants have chosen to be non-Jewish. These were Jews—Jews integrally involved in the American experience, with a place in the nation's history that should never be denied or forgotten. They were road builders, Indian traders, land agents, ferry operators, innkeepers, gunsmiths, bankers, lawyers, doctors, soldiers and sheriffs. It is a proud heritage, one that should be cherished by us all.

Elzina Grimwood carried more than one secret to the grave. To everyone's surprise, including her surviving brother's, her will stipulated she be buried in the Ramey family crypt, which she had paid for and maintained for more than sixty years. Everyone assumed she would join the other Grimwoods in their family burial grounds. When the cemetery authorities opened the specified grave in the old Ramey plot they found the skeleton of a young man. No one knew who he was.

Shortly before his own death, my father-in-law called my wife over to his house to cart off a box of treasured belongings his sister had left him.

Among the records was a large parchment scroll of the Ramey genealogy. Back through Tennessee, back through Virginia, back through England and France, it displayed Elzina's ancestry in a careful, round schoolteacher's writing.

The Rameys were Jews from ancient Rome and Alexandrine Egypt, originally from Israel.

Julia

5 CRAZY QUILT ANCESTRY

This article is republished from Melungeons.com, March 2008, "European Tapestries, Middle Eastern Kilims, &
Appalachian Quilts: The Weaving of America."

Some trips we take are of the mind and not the body. Sometimes all you know about yourself, or think you know about yourself, changes or gets such additions as to make the picture different enough to feel like a change. It's amazing how the catalyst for such a moment can be something as simple as a clipping from a newspaper.

In 2002 my mother sent me a copy of a clipping from the Kingsport *Times-News* because it mentioned a friend from my school days. "I thought you and Billy might be interested in reading this," Mother had written in blue ink across the article, right under the title, "Solving a puzzle to relieve the pain." She thought our only interest would be in the fact that the article featured someone that we'd known. I don't think that she realized that she had set my feet upon a path that would carry my family and me to the other side of the world and back again.

I found the article to be of interest for a very different reason from the one my mother had thought would interest me. It was my first introduction to Brent Kennedy and to the term familial Mediterranean fever (FMF).

For as long as I can remember, I have never felt very well. There are days that it's a challenge to put one foot in front of the other. My daughter Julia says that some days you operate on the principal of "might as well." As in, "I'm up, so I might as well do what needs doing," she says. I read that article and I heard every ache and every complaint I'd ever had in it. I was driven to learn more, but the more I learned the more there was to know.

I bought Brent's book, *The Melungeons: The Resurrection of a Proud People,* because I wanted to know more about how he came to be diagnosed with FMF—a genetic disorder found most often in people of non-Ashkenazi Jewish, Armenian, Arab and Turkish backgrounds. As I was reading the book I kept thinking that his family names sounded so familiar. A look at a family tree that had been kept up away from sight revealed that Brent's ancestors were the brothers, sisters and cousins to my own ancestors. If nothing else—I had found a new cousin.

My mystery illness might finally have a name! Armed with the newspaper clipping, my family tree and Brent's book I returned to my primary physician. A few months earlier in a state of frustration at not being able to find a reason for all my aches and pains he had at last said, "Don't come back, Phyllis; there's nothing I can do for you." On the basis that I was related to Brent and had suffered the same symptoms, my doctor gave me a referral to Dr. Christopher Morris in Kingsport, Tennessee, who had been mentioned in the article. I think he figured that this might at last put a name to my condition or at least prove that it was "all in my head. "

I found out in my appointment with Dr. Morris that diagnosing Familial Mediterranean Fever is often a process of eliminating anything else that might explain the symptoms. There has to be the genetic connection—at that point to Brent and some few other patients that had also been diagnosed—and then all the tests to eliminate other illnesses that have similar symptoms. Once the other possible culprits are eliminated then a trial of colchicine could be prescribed. A positive reaction to the medication is a positive indicator of FMF.

I have been taking colchicine for six years now. There are still days that are challenging, but the episodes of joint pain, sore throat, low grade fevers, pleurisy and unexplained abdominal pain are less frequent and shorter in duration than before my introduction to it. My husband and two of three children are also taking colchicine. It has made life better for all of us. Only someone who has suffered a nameless condition can ever truly appreciate how it feels just to have a name for what ails you. It's not enough to know the what, though; I had to know the how. How could a family from southwest Virginia be diagnosed with a condition for which there was no connection to our known origins?

This was the start of my travels down paper trails, to county courthouses, family reunions with people I hardly knew or didn't know at all. The names keep multiplying as I go back through time tracking generations. Adams, Berry, Beverly, Bowling, Campbell, Carter, Caudill, Cole, Counts, Cox, Coxe, Fields, Freeman, Gibson, Hill, Jackson, Kiser, Lawson, Lucas, Mosely, Mullins, Osborn, Osborne, Powers, Pruitt, Rasnick, Robinson, Shephard, Short, Stallard, Stanley, Stewart, Taylor, Tipton, Turner, Williams, Williamson and others.

My family has lived by and played in and on the banks of the Clinch River and Stony Creek for generations—the same Stony Creek where the old Primitive Baptist church of the same name once stood—the same Stony Creek church that is often put forth as the place where the earliest known written reference to the word "melungins" occurred in 1813. The listing of membership from that time is a "Who's Who" of mine and my husband's family trees. The original church building was washed away by floods a long time ago. My husband's family and my mother were members at the Pine Grove church that replaced it. My mother sometimes took my daughters to services there when they stayed with her during summer breaks. It was still a one room church house with a curtain to pull for Sunday school, and an outhouse. Baptisms were still performed in the deep spot right behind it in Stony Creek—the same deep spot that served as a swimming hole on Saturdays.

Our family trees have long and deep roots; I am still following threads here and there trying to sort them out. The roots and branches are intertwined so that in some places it's hard to tell where one tree ends and the other begins. I have reached some ends that I can no longer follow. I am sometimes like a squirrel whose weight bears down on the branch too much so that I must leap to another one for a while. My search has led me to counties outside of Scott County, Virginia such as Lee, Wise, Russell, Dickenson, Patrick, Louisa and Cumberland, Virginia. I have crossed the border to Tennessee to Hawkins, Hancock, Grainger, Greene, Claiborne, Sullivan and Washington Counties. I've made trips to Letcher, Perry, and Clay county. Kentucky chasing down a name or a possible ancestor. I have found that at some point the paper trail runs thin—fires, floods and politics can be blamed for records being lost or destroyed. In all of the trails that I can follow this way, I still hadn't found out how a Southeastern Appalachian family could possibly have a Mediterranean medical disorder.

My husband and I attended the Fourth Union hosted by the Melungeon Heritage Association (MHA) in Kingsport in 2002, right after I had first visited with Dr. Morris. I had only been taking colchicine for a few weeks at that point. This was the event where the preliminary results of the first Melungeon DNA project were announced by Dr. Kevin Jones. It is unfortunate that project wasn't able to be followed to its end due to Dr. Jones' illness, but this event did have some lasting effects for my family in a personal way. I met Cousin Brent and found cousins Beth (Caldwell Hirschman), Donald (Panther-Yates) and Nancy

(Sparks Morrison), among others; although, at the time I didn't realize that they were my cousins. Their research has added to that of my own and we have all been able to fill in pieces of the puzzles that we have been working to put together individually. Subsequent MHA events for many years have been like extended family reunions.

The first time I ever saw Donald Panther-Yates, before he'd even spoken, I told my husband, "I don't know who he is, but I want to pick his brain." Once I heard him speak at Fourth Union—his topic, "Jewish Indian: Who'd 've Thunk It!" —I knew he was right. If you've ever had an epiphany—a moment when you KNOW the truth when you've heard it, this was one of those moments. I had never thought about it. It can only happen if you are willing to accept the possibilities—I was willing to accept this new aspect as to who my ancestors might have been: Jewish, Muslim, Christian, Native American, Mediterranean, Middle Eastern, Romani, Northern African, as well as northern European. I went from being a white, middle class Appalachian American to multi-racial. It was a huge leap and yet I am so much richer for having made it.

My family doesn't look any different from everyone I grew up with in Fort Blackmore, Virginia. At one point in history, though, a Virginia state official apparently thought that families with my ancestors' surnames were different enough to warrant being treated differently. Did Walter Plecker cause some members of my family to "whitewash" the family lore? At what point in time did my Native

American ancestors decide not to be Native American? Why did my Romani ancestors decide that they weren't Roma? When did my Mediterranean forefathers and mothers decide that they had to be the same as their neighbors? The truth is lost irretrievably from the prospective of paper records and my family lore has long since forgotten the answers to any of these questions. I now had more clues about our origins, but how to prove it? Science provided me with another avenue to follow. Where a door closes, often a window opens.

The new and upcoming thing in genealogy for a few years now has been the use of genetic and DNA technologies. Once I accepted that the paper trail was never going to go back far enough to find my family's origins or to explain our medical condition, I decided that this new path was the only one that might possibly provide the links. Paper trails can definitely be lies; blood trails don't lie but neither can they always be taken at face value and some results only create more questions. We chose to support Donald's new venture, DNA Consultants, and ordered the mtDNA test for myself and both the Y-DNA and mtDNA test for my husband. My husband's Y-DNA results showed an Albanian or Macedonian modal (R1b). His mtDNA results (T*) had an exact match in Iceland. My mtDNA came back U2e, which is normally considered a European haplogroup, but I have no HVS1 matches and my HVS2 region matches that of a documented Cherokee woman. Answers? Yes. Questions? Yes.

I have continued to chase down paper trails,

but my thirst for knowledge has not been quenched. A new type of DNA testing has become feasible for public consumption—autosomal testing has become affordable. DNA Consultants offers a DNA ethnotyping test—which matches CODIS markers to contemporary populations. It is the same test used to match evidence to victims or suspects in crimes. It is the same test that is used to prove maternity and paternity. The numbers alone won't give you much information; the profile and map provided with the test answers many questions. They also gave me new topics to research—I've found it interesting that many of our individual matches can be connected through historical events and shared borders. I have at this point had a few of my maternal and paternal family members tested as well as my husband, my three daughters and one grandchild. My family's common matches show that we are, indeed, of northern European descent—with many members having matches in the United Kingdom, France, several Scandinavian countries and the Iberian Peninsula. However, this wasn't the whole story, as the history books would have us believe.

We also had common matches in Morocco, Tunisia, Syria, Saudi Arabia, Turkey, Greece and Afghanistan to name a few Middle Eastern matches. Every family member had at least two or more of these countries on their matches and the matches occurred for at least three or more members. There are also matches in several scattered countries including northern India that would indicate a Romani or Gypsy ancestry. There were even some Australian aboriginal matches and some Sub-Saharan African matches.

What may be the most recent additions to the family history are our numerous Native American matches—the top or second match of many family members being a Lumbee or North Carolina Native American match. There are other Native American matches all over North, Central and South America. None of these can be interpreted as a specific tribal affiliation, because native DNA does not easily break down according to tribe or even region.

I have at least proven that it's possible for me to suffer from Familial Mediterranean Fever. I have the ethnic backgrounds most often affected in my genetic makeup. If for no other reason, the decision to have my DNA tested was worth knowing/proving this to be the case. There is one thing that anyone thinking about taking this path should consider—it may disprove as easily as it may prove any stories of origin that your family may have. I do not think that I would have gotten as much out of it, if I hadn't been willing to accept all the possibilities.

Will I ever track down which ancestors came from where exactly? Most likely not, because I think many of the ancestors that you could say came from here or there are probably hundreds of years back. I believe that most of the mixing of various ethnicities happened before my ancestors came to the Americas. I now believe that I have ancestors that were here prior to those that I know came before or during the Revolutionary War. I am more firmly than ever an Appalachian American. And I am also Native American, northern

European, Mediterranean, Middle Eastern and Romani (Gypsy). And yet since my ancestors chose (perhaps freely, perhaps out of necessity) to become Anglo-American—I am none of these things. I sometimes feel like I am an "orphan of the world." I know that many people from the cultures and heritages that are a part of me wouldn't accept me as a part of them.

It seems to be human nature to want to label and categorize things—including people. It is most definitely human nature to want to belong and to be accepted. I think the greatest challenge in being a multi-racial person in a time when society is supposedly more enlightened is resisting pressure to choose to acknowledge one facet of your heritage over the others in order to wear a certain label. That pressure comes from those that are uncomfortable with you defying their attempt to put you in one category or keep you out of another. It seems to me that if I reject one part of myself to satisfy anyone's desire to label me or appease my own longing to belong then I repeat history. I start down the same slippery slope that some ancestor slid down long ago. I hope not to repeat the decision that I consider in the present to have been a mistake in the past.

It is my hope that one day the world will be able to accept the diversity that makes up the foundations of America. It is my hope that one day the average American will recognize that our history is much deeper than what we thought it was. I think that groups like the Melungeon Heritage Association are the best way to start. If we can hold to the belief that the purpose of the MHA is to celebrate the richness of culture and the diversity of heritage that is Appalachia—if we can keep to the belief that we are "one people, all colors," then we stand the best chance of finding a sense of belonging and feeling of acceptance for how we are different. We will finally be able to be true to ourselves. The beauty of Appalachia's people is that we are much like a tapestry, a kilim or a quilt—it takes many threads of many colors to make a whole.

Stech-tcha-kó-me-co, Great King
(called Ben Perryman), a Chief

6 WHO'DA THUNK IT

Remarks for Melungeon 4ᵗʰ Union, Kingsport, Tennessee, June 20-22, 2002, "Jewish Indian: Who'da Thunk It!" by Donald Panther-Yates

A turn-of-the-century Jewish Austrian insurance clerk named Franz Kafka wrote some rather bizarre fiction. You may have come across one of his pieces which is heavily anthologized, called "The Metamorphosis." It tells the story of a man who wakes up one morning to find that he has been changed into a gigantic cockroach. His mother and sister come after him with a broom and drive him out of the bedroom.

When I first learned that my family was Jewish—and what is even more fantastic, Jewish-Indian—I felt like I had suddenly entered one of Kafka's surrealistic short stories. I felt like the cosmos had played an enormous joke on me. I was mad at my mother, father, aunts, uncles and grandparents for not cueing me in. After hearing from Kevin Jones and Beth Hirschman many of you are probably in the same boat.

I'm going to speak to you today on the subject of early intermarriage of Sephardic Jews and Indians and the contributions Jews made to Indian society and, through Indians, to American civilization as a whole.

I *could* say that I believe my family history — incredible as it is — is typical of many others. I *won't* say that it is indicative of all Melungeons, or of all Southeastern Indians, or of all Jews, not by any means. I *will* say though that I think it is instructive, and that I feel comfortable sharing these things with you here at 4th Union as part of a great, big family. We are perhaps the largest extended family in history to wake up one day with a new genetic identity. It is exciting to be part of this moment of destiny, one that forces us to rethink our individual identities, our family's traditions and our roles as Americans.

About five years ago, I wrote a genealogy essay for an e-mail discussion group I moderated on Rootsweb called "Indian Tribes Southeast." The title of the piece was "Seven Generations of Cherokee Blood." One of my findings was that part-Cherokee had consistently married part-Cherokee, even when the marriage partner came from rather far away and outside the other's locale, effectively conserving the bloodline. Rather being thinned down by out-marriage, my Cherokee heritage on both my mother's side and my father's — the Coopers and the Yateses — remained fairly constant at about one-quarter from generation to generation. For instance, a quarter-blood Cooper would marry a quarter-blood Blevins and their children would all be quarter-bloods. I postulated that the effect was not accidental, though I could not explain the motives behind it. Well, I was right and wrong.

The phenomenon I observed was cousin marriage among crypto-Jews. It is why there are only about two hundred Melungeon surnames and we are all multiply related. The purpose was to keep business affairs and religious practices safely concealed within the family — free from the imputations and exposure of outsiders who might jeopardize the family's standing and rights in the community. Since our ancestors lived in closely-knit communities, the degree of secrecy and forgiveness for speaking out of school was extremely strict and severe. Remember they had been at this for five hundred years or more, staying one step ahead of the Spanish Inquisition by a combination of tried-and-true policies and exacting discipline. In medieval and early modern Spain, often only one child in the family would be told of the Jewish heritage, and sometimes there was not one son or daughter deemed worthy of keeping the secret.

The book *The Jews of Georgian England* has a revealing anecdote about a London tradesman who appeared before a court of law. The judge was completely exasperated because the man would admit to being neither a Jew nor a non-Jew. Since different laws applied to Jews, it was important to know. It is unlikely that the man was ignorant that he was a Jew, yet later on instances abound, especially in America, where people only find out about their Jewish background more or less by accident. In Appalachia, there came a point where a generation gap occurred. Either the parents and grandparents did not think it necessary to tell or the children did not think it necessary to ask. There was wide-scale neglect of traditions. The Melungeons became mysteries even to themselves.

In the meantime, families explained their "differentness" as Black Dutch, Black Irish, Indian or Portuguese—anything but what it truly was. In my family, the exotic looks were explained as coming from a great-grandmother Shankles' Indian blood. She didn't even have a first name. She was supposedly three-quarters Cherokee Indian. Sometimes the story became completely illogical, as when the children of Nancy Cooper were said to be "two-thirds" Choctaw in one of my family's Bibles. Everything was put on my mother's side of the family, though I later discovered my mother and father had practically the same gene type. My mother's father said all the Indian blood was on his wife's side. I later found out they both had about the same amount and were in fact fourth cousins. I kept trying to push my lines back to reach the fullbloods but never quite succeeded. Have you ever noticed how many people only have one Indian in the family? Well, I don't believe Indians come that way. They each must have two Indian parents. I also reject the notion that Indian genes entered a predominantly white bloodline by some sort of aberration, an occurrence of rape or an adoption or a kidnapping. Our mixed ancestor couples formed successful marriages of mutual choice and love, often producing ten or eleven children.

So let us survey the different Southeastern Indian tribes, or nations, and try to answer the question when the first intermarriages occurred. That first generation's children would have been exactly half Indian. The first tribe I will talk about is the Chickasaw. From the earliest English contact with them, which dates from the end of the seventeenth century, this powerful tribe of Muskogean-speaking Indians dominating the bluffs on the Mississippi around Memphis was called the Halfbreeds. This name was used in preference to Chickasaw by the Board of Commissioners of Indian Trade in Charleston and the Lord High Commissioners in London. Among present-day Indians in Oklahoma the Chickasaw are rumored to be the most highly mixed, "virtually white," as one Indian put it to me. About 1735 the tribe was invited to settle in the hinterland of the new colony of Savannah where they owned thousands of acres on both sides of the Savannah River around Augusta complete with plantations until after the American Revolution. The Chickasaw were resolutely anti-Spanish and anti-French, and it is likely that the first white people among them were Jews. The French finance minister in the early eighteenth century was a Scotsman, William Law (whose name is Hebrew, "Levite"). Law introduced paper money and government bonds to that country. One of his schemes—today we would call it junk bonds—was the Mississippi Bubble of 1718. It involved rounding up the poor of Paris along with the Jews and Gypsies who lived in Alsace and sending several shiploads of colonists up the Mississippi. The land agent was Elias Stultheus, a Jew. These unlikely soldiers of fortune were essentially dumped among the Indians, without guns to defend themselves, and they later disappeared. It may be this colony that the Choctaw chief Apunkshunnubbee referred to in the 1790s when he told the Indian agent concerning the upper Natchez territory:

"You Americans were not the first people who got this country from the red people. We sold our lands, but never got any value for it."

(Alternatively, this may be a memory of the "gentlemen who came to view Mississippi lands from the Yadkin River in North Carolina," as mentioned by Adair. The infamous Yazoo Land Fraud and Aaron Burr conspiracy did not occur until after this.)

The Indian trader James Adair moved his base of operations to the village of Piomingo in north Mississippi around 1745. Most of his arguments involving similarities between the Indians and Jews were founded on information he received in Chickasaw country. He wrote his *History of the American Indians* there in the 1760s. He says on page 447, "I have the pleasure of writing this by the side of a Chikkasah female, as great a princess as ever lived." Here we have explicit mention of the first Jewish American Indian Princess! Adair noted that there were already adults who were octoroons, or one-eighth Indian. This would necessarily mean that the first Indian-white intermarriage occurred three generations before about 1680, allowing 20 years per generation.

By 1800, after the area had returned to the Spanish, there was just one town of Halfbreeds left. It is mentioned in the memoirs of a steamboat captain below the fourth bluffs on the Mississippi:

"Fort Pickering...stands on the left side of the river, in the Mississippi Territory. The United States have a factor here, but the settlement is very then; it generally consists of what is called the half breed, which is a mixture of Indians and whites" (*The Navigator*, by Zadok Cramer, 1811).

The author of the article on Jews in the *Encyclopedia of Southern Culture* says that the oldest Southern communities were not on the Atlantic or Gulf coast but in the middle Mississippi river valley on the St. Francis and Arkansas River, in outposts originally Spanish or French like Natchez, New Madrid, Kaskaskia, Cape Giroudeau and Memphis. These are all Jewish ghost towns now, like so many of the Caribbean Islands where the first synagogues in the New World were built. Today there are only twenty-five Jews in the city of Natchez. The Museum of the Southern Jewish Experience in Utica, Mississippi, is a lonely tribute to the state's Jewish pioneers.

What about white surnames among the Chickasaw? The Colberts had tremendous influence over the Chickasaws. The family practically ruled them for many years. They owned land, had plantations, slaves, ferry operations, credit in Pensacola, Cadiz, Amsterdam and London, their women wore the latest fashions from Paris, and they maintained libraries and wine cellars. The first of their ilk was William Colbert, a British Indian trader from the Carolinas who visited the Chickasaw as early as 1722. His son was Chief James Lachlan Colbert, one of whose three wives was a halfbreed woman. Chief James's sons were Chief William who married a Moniac and lived among the Creeks; Chief George, who operated Colberts Ferry where the Natchez Trace crosses the Tennessee River (he became very wealthy); Levi, who lived nearby at Buzzards Roost (Franklin County, Alabama); and Joseph, who was the family historian. "Colbert" became a famous boy's name among Jewish Indians in the South. I leave it to you to decide whether the Colberts were Jewish, and if so, how much. If we look at the names of the operators of the first stands on the Natchez Trace—in other words the first white men in that part of the country—the majority of them can be suspected of being Jewish by background, including Stephen Minor, Louis LeFleur, John Gordon, Robert Griner, Levi Kemp and Noah Wall. Significantly, perhaps, the earliest name given to this region by the Cumberland settlers in Nashville was Moro District—the "Moorish District."

Let us go now to the Choctaw Indians. Chief Greenwood Leflore (1800-1865) was one of the signers of the Treaty of Dancing Rabbit Creek that cost the Choctaws their homeland. Ironically, he promoted removal to his people (for which he became unpopular), but he remained in Mississippi, an immensely wealthy man. He even served on the Mississippi state senate 1841-1844. He also built a magnificent home, Malmaison, near what is now Teoc, Mississippi. Greenberry's father was Louis LeFleur, a French Canadian trader who married an "Indian princess" by the name of

Rebecca Cravatt. LeFleur was responsible for the fact that the capital of Mississippi is in Jackson, where his trading post and plantation was situated.

Another of the first white traders among the Choctaws (as early as 1767) was Hardy Perry, father of Chief Isaac Perry. Hardy Perry operated a trading post near present-day Tupelo after coming into the territory from Georgia. Reportedly he was the first to introduce oxen into the Choctaw Nation, bringing the animals north from Mobile. He had a Choctaw wife named Anolah, who lived near present-day Grenada, Mississippi, and also a wife in the neighboring Chickasaw Nation. Here we are obviously dealing with crypto-Jews. The Perrys were a Sephardic family whose name (Perez) was Biblical and originally, according to legend, paid tribute to the pear tree of Eretz Israel. Probably the same family is the namesake for Parris Island, where the last of Juan Pardo's settlers were found. Anolah, we can be sure, was not a fullblood. At any rate, her name (whose origin is obscure) became famous with the "Enola Gay," the jet fortress that dropped the atomic bomb on Hiroshima. Perry is the same name as Perryman. The Sephardic features are, I think, very striking in the portrait of Benjamin Perryman, a Creek warrior.

In 1898, a famous case was brought before the Choctaw supreme court in Indian Territory, Nancy Cooper v. The Choctaw Nation. This was followed by an even more famous case, William C. Thompson et al. vs. The Choctaw Nation. Involved were the Indian citizenship claims of hundreds of mixed blood descendants of the earliest traders among the Choctaw and Chickasaw Indians. After the cases were accepted and favorably adjudicated by the Indian courts they were overturned by the BIA. The Thompson case went as high as the U.S. Supreme Court, but none of the plaintiffs ever got any satisfaction. The Thompson Choctaws of East Texas are still today a viable tribe. Among the names in the Cooper case—all considered Melungeon—were Boen or Bowen, Campbell, Martin, Brown and Nichols.

One of my earliest named Cooper ancestors was Henry Labon Cooper. He is said to have been a Choctaw Indian, spoke the Choctaw language and had typical Choctaw Indian looks according to witnesses. One of his sons, Capt. John Cooper signed the Treaty of Dancing Rabbit Creek and went on the Trail of Tears, forfeiting a large plantation in Perry County, Tennessee. Another, Houston Cooper, managed to remain on his plantation outside Nashville, although married to an octoroon woman (that is, one-eighth Indian). Another, my third great-grandfather, Isaac Cooper, married Nancy, daughter of Cherokee supreme chief Black Fox. For many years, he lived on his grandfather William Cooper's place on Copper Ridge (which I think was probably originally Cooper Ridge) in Grainger County, Tennessee, near William Bean's lonely log cabin, the first built west of the Cumberland Gap.

This brings me to the Sephardic Jews among the Cherokee Indians. William and Joseph Cooper, brothers with a shop on the harborfront in early Charleston, are the first known English traders among the Cherokee. They are documented as early as 1698. They had a trading post in Keowee where their mother lived in 1730, and they accompanied the eccentric Scotsman Sir Alexander Cummings on his mission to win the "crown of Tennessee" for King George. Interestingly, Cummings' idea was to settle 300,000 European Jews in the mountains of the Cherokees. It was probably his Jewish connections rather than his aristocratic airs that made him persona non grata when he brought seven Cherokee Indians over to London in 1730—including Attakullakulla, my fifth great-grandfather. William Cooper was, like many Jewish merchants, a linguister or translator. It is thought that the Coopers were originally retainers who came over to England from France with William the Conqueror and went underground with their beliefs when the Jews were expelled from England in 1290. The most famous member of the family was Anthony Ashley-Cooper, 1st earl of Shaftesbury and Lord Proprietor of the Carolinas under Charles II. James Fenimore Cooper's ancestors were also a branch of this family, settled in Barbados, Philadelphia and New York.

About the same time, the Beamor family came from Barbados and Colleton County, South Carolina (where they were allied with the Perryman family—namesakes of the Purrysborough colony) and began to trade with the Cherokee. Brent Cox, the author of *The Heart of the Eagle*, a study of Dragging Canoe's Chickamauga movement, shows that John Beamor married Quatsi (whose name means Patsy, just as Qualla is Cherokee for Polly), the Wolf Clan mother of the entire Cherokee leadership for most of the eighteenth century, including Oconostota ("the

Great Warrior"), the various children of Moytoy, Doublehead and Attakullakulla. The Cherokee hierarchy responsible for signing all the treaties with England and the United States was thus mixed in its roots from the beginning. A case can be made that all the well-known founders of old Cherokee families, from MacDonald and Ward to Ross and Gist, as presented, for instance, in Emmett Starr's work or James Hicks' Cherokee Genealogy pages on the Internet, were Sephardic Jews. A rather obvious example, in my opinion, is Col. George Lowrey. Two others from my own family are Moses Looney and Melmuth Lackey.

I will be brief about the Creeks and Seminoles. The most important founder of Jewish-Indian trading families among the Creeks was William Dixon Moniac (originally Jacob Monaque "from Munich"), who married Polly Colbert, a cousin, the daughter of Chief William Colbert and Jesse Moniac. Dixon Moniac was said to be a Hollander but was originally from France. He came to the Tallassee Creeks with a remnant of the Natchez Indians in 1756. His son was Sam Moniac, a plantation and innkeeper on the Alabama River in southwest Alabama called "a halfbreed of property" by the government. His son-in-law was William Weatherford, or Red Eagle, the hero of the Creek war. A granddaughter married William Sizemore. The Moniacs rallied the handful of names that became the Poarch Creek Band in the 1980s, on the strength of a dusty Spanish charter preserved by the Pensacola firm of Panton, Leslie. The main names were Sizemore, Elliott (Ehlert), McGhee, Tate, Grayson/Grierson, Powell,

Perryman, McIntosh, Barnard and Weatherford.

The Moniac blood blended with that of another legendary founder, James McQueen, who lived to be 128 years old and was the grandfather of Tecumseh, Osceola and Josiah Francis (Hillis Harjo). McQueen was a British naval officer who jumped ship in Pensacola harbor in 1719. He married a succession of Creek princesses. Most of the so-called Breeds among both the Upper and Lower Creeks were his children or grandchildren or great-grandchildren. McQueen is one of the oldest clans in Scotland and it was probably founded by a Cohen, as one of its septs is Cowan. So we see that the common denominator in Creek genealogies is also Jewish.

Osceola, one of the greatest of the Creek chiefs, was born about 1804 in a village near the Tallapoosa River in Alabama. His people were called Tallassees, but his father was believed to have been a half-breed Scottish-Creek trader named William Powell. In the Creek and Seminole Wars, Osceola was captured in Florida and imprisoned at Fort Moultrie on Sullivan's Island in Charleston, South Carolina, where he died on January 30, 1838. The shameful story of his capture, death and subsequent decapitation has been told many times.

Josiah Francis, or Hillis Hadjo, was another Creek leader, born about 1770. Known as The Prophet to the Creeks, he was son of an Indian mother and an English father. His father, David Francis, was a trader and silversmith, who lived many years in Autauga Town and specialized in making ornaments and medallions to be awarded to chiefs by the government. Josiah was a cousin of Tecumseh. It is probable that their kinship was through their white ancestry rather than through their Indian lines. He was also half-brother of Sam Moniac.

The story of white-Indian relations in North America has most often been told as one gigantic unfolding theft. Angie Debo, Vine Deloria and A. Alvarez are some of its better-known chroniclers. Guilt, anger, deception and misunderstanding dominate among the emotions. European colonists took the red man's lives, land, livelihood, language and culture; they are even trying today to rob the Indian of his spirituality and identity. But the Sephardic Jewish colonists, whose roots were in North Africa, consistently went against this pattern. Where their English and Spanish counterparts did little more than take, the Jews and Moors gave. They gave large families of children, leadership abilities, trading relationships, writing and computational skills, building and construction know-how, legal advice, spinning wheels, looms, forges, smithies, ferries, cows, horses, peach orchards, beautiful arts and crafts. In the case of Will Thomas, they even gave land, for he endowed the Eastern Band of Cherokee Indians with their present-day reservation in North Carolina.

The Five Civilized Tribes built an amazing legacy, one that endures to this day as strong as ever. After the 2000 Census, the Cherokee constitute the largest Indian group in the U.S., with nearly 500,000 recognized and unrecognized members. Through genocide, military conquest, plague, starvation, captivity, dispossession, betrayal and endless government maneuvers, they and the other major Southeastern tribes fought back with cunning and conviction. These were the first Indian nations to have constitutions, courts of law, a press, police forces and schools. Euchella v. Welsh (1824) and the Cherokee case before the U.S. Supreme Court in the 1830s marked their arrival in the circle of nations. The ensuing public sympathy stirred up by converted Jews like John Howard Payne, the author of "Home Sweet Home," secured a place in legend for them similar to the Founding Fathers of America and Davy Crockett.

Families like the McDonalds, Adairs, Rosses, Coopers, Keyses, Browns, Rogerses and Vanns — many of whose names may now pass for Melungeon — mingled their bloodlines with the strength of the natives. Were it not for that leaven, the Cherokee, Chickasaw, Creek and Choctaw could never have survived as political entities. Were it not for that intermarriage, most Southeastern Indians would not have acquired immunities to disease and survived at all. Southern Sephardic Jews were the straw in a bricklike material formed in the crucible of the Old Frontier. Flexible, down-to-earth, inconspicuous, they infiltrated and inspired the indigenous hierarchies. Almost all traces of them have eroded away with time, but DNA is uncovering their amazing and enduring story.

The old chief and his
assistant gave us
a fraternal handshake.

7 INFLUENCE OF SEPHARDIC JEWS AND MOORS ON SOUTHEASTERN INDIANS

Keynote address given at the annual meeting of the Institute for the Study of American Cultures, Columbus, Georgia, October 2002

Since the 1980s, I have felt that my life imitated the fiction of Bernard Malamud, who wrote in one of his books about the strange career of Chief Jozip, described as a "half-ass white Indian." I discovered I was descended from Choctaw and Cherokee chiefs after being raised to believe that I was Scots-Irish and English. I became the band chief of the New York and New Jersey Cherokees when I lived in Princeton. I taught at the Native College in Chicago when I lived there. I ran a public relations agency for indigenous rights work in Nashville. When I turned fifty, I became an elder of the Thunderbird Clan of the Teehahnahmah People in

Tennessee. And most recently—and perhaps most surprisingly— found out through DNA testing I am Sephardic Jewish.

My fourth-great-grandfather married a daughter of the last great Cherokee chief, Black Fox. His grandfather, William Cooper, had participated in the founding of an important Jewish colony in Daniel Boone's Kentucky. The Coopers can be traced back to medieval France and the duchy of Toulouse. Like the royal Stuart family, they were retainers in the court of William the Conqueror, also Knights Templar and Levites. I can't say the Cooper line was an isolated case either. Y-chromosome testing proved that most of the surnames in my family tree were Sephardic Jewish. It was all of a piece. I was, quite simply, a Jewish Indian, approximately an eighth to tenth-generation one, to boot!

I'm going to speak to you today about the influence of Sephardic Jews—one of the two divisions of world Jewry—on Indian cultures in the Southeast U.S. The time frame is approximately 1600 to 1800. The area was predominantly Spanish and the first contact took place between the tribes of the interior and traders from the coastal settlements of St. Augustine, Savannah, Jamestown and Pensacola. My conclusions are—funny as it may sound—that the five so-called "Civilized Tribes" of the Cherokee, Choctaw, Chickasaw, Creek and Seminole owe their high degree of assimilation, long history of treaty-making, trade and legal rights, and in fact their very survival to Sephardic Jews like my forefather Isaac Cooper. It is not true that the Indians of North America are descendants of the lost tribes of Israel, but it is true that the earliest Jewish travelers and the indigenous people they visited and chose to settle among had many things in common. Relations between the two races were probably promoted by the mistaken belief on both sides that they were historically and genetically related. Whatever the implications of this wrong notion may have been, the Jewish descent of Indians was accepted on a popular level and also on a scientific level until quite recently. In the interests of condensing a large amount of material into the short span of thirty minutes here at the ISAC conference, I will concentrate on three arguments to show the degree of inter-influence between Jews and Indians. The three arguments are the identity and importance of the Melungeons, the ancient history of North American reflected in what is called Indian seer tradition and certain chiefs' genealogies.

My first argument has to do with Melungeons. They have been called a "triracial Appalachian isolate," and their origins have, until recently, been one of the longstanding mysteries in American history. Nearly every surname in my family tree— as also in my wife's— is a Melungeon name. There are about 200 identified as such. Several substantive books have been written about this ethnic group, each building upon the prior ones to identify their origins.

Among the most popular and well-documented theories are (1) that the Melungeons are survivors of Sir Walter Raleigh's "Lost Colony" of Roanoke, (2) that the Melungeons are descendents of early Spanish and Portuguese sailors marooned or "dumped" in the Carolinas, and (3) that the Melugeons are the descendents of *converso* Moors and Jews who fled the Inquisition. In 2003, the Mercer University Press in nearby Macon will publish Dr. Elizabeth Hirschman's breakthrough study, *Melungeons: The Last Lost Tribe in America.* I was fortunate to read the work in manuscript and become a collaborator with Hirschman, who is a marketing professor at Rutgers University specializing in the impact of ethnicity on consumer behavior. Using a combination of Y chromosome testing, genealogy and local history, Hirschman has proved beyond the shadow of a doubt that the forebears of the Melungeons were Sephardic Jews. Among her quite brilliant discoveries are that Daniel Boone, David Crockett, Andrew Jackson, Jefferson Davis, Abraham Lincoln, Sam Houston and James Robertson, the founder of the Cumberland settlements in Tennessee, all came from Jewish ancestry.

It is a stunning revelation to find out that many of the earliest settlers in Virginia, West Virginia, North Carolina, Georgia, South Carolina, Florida, Kentucky and Tennessee were not brave, white-skinned Anglo-Saxons and Celts from the British Isles (in other words, Christians), but rather dusky, dark-eyed, dark haired, exotic Semites and Berbers from North Africa and Spain. It was Moors who occupied Black-a-moor's fort on the Clinch River; it was a Semitic Daniel Boone who cleared the path through the Cumberland Gap into Kentucky. This knowledge challenges not only our view of American history, but also the modern image of Jews and Muslims.

How ironic to think that these two peoples, whom we usually hear about shooting each other on the West Bank and Gaza Strip, or exporting oil, or working on Wall Street, were—450 years ago— trudging together inland toward the Appalachian Mountains. They were soon intermarrying, reproducing, becoming Primitive and Old Regular Baptists, going to Freemason meetings, riding horses, shooting rifles, salting hogs, growing corn and tobacco, fighting the British at King's Mountain and fighting both the Yankees and the Rebels during the Civil War.

Last June at the biennial 4th Melungeon Union in Kingsport, Tennessee, the results were released of a long-awaited two-year study by Kevin Jones on the genetic diversity of a core group of self-identifying Melungeons, most of whom came from Newmans Ridge or nearby Wise, Virginia. The findings confirmed there were haplotypes with matches in Syria, Turkey, Arabia and other Mediterranean lands, and there were some rare genes with no matches anywhere. One surprise was a female line that came from the Siddhis, the descendants of Africans brought to India as slaves and thought to be related to the Untouchables and Gypsies. In general, 5% of the gene pool was Native American, 5% was African American and 90% was Eurasian. It was pointed out, however, that these results did not markedly differ from the surrounding population. Nevertheless, the founder figures of the Melungeons must have included both males and females, or family units. In other words, the ethnic group called the Melungeons could not be explained as the progeny of shipwrecked sailors, runaway slaves and renegade soldiers taking up with Indian women (some of the prevailing views). I believe we can trace here the deliberate migration of Jewish couples. These Jews, however motivated and organized, planted a secretive Marrano culture in the Appalachians, one that has only begun to fade in our grandparents' generation.

In addition what we might call the Melungeon Pilgrim Fathers and Mothers, there was evidently also a certain amount of intermarriage with American Indians. The unusual case of the Sizemore tribe of Indians—another big Melungeon name—proves that it was not always a lonely Sephardic or Moorish sailor or soldier taking an Indian bride. Sizemore male DNA matches American Indians of Panama, Alaska and the American Southwest. We can only infer that sometimes a Eurasian woman picked an Indian man for her mate. The Melungeon argument shows us that the most important influence Jews and Moors had on southeastern Indians was in selecting them for trade, marriage and worship partners.

But why did Sephardic Jews landing in Baltimore or marooned in the Carolinas automatically head for Kentucky and Tennessee? What thought processes naturally put Cherokee and Jew together? My second argument comes from Indian seer tradition, a body of oral teachings propagated by the members of medicine societies such as the Midewewin Lodge. Many of its stories were passed to me by Paul Russell, a Potawatomi-Shawnee-Yuchi-Cherokee elder in Tennessee also known as Two White Feathers. Before sharing with you some of this lore, I want to say a few words about the value and social function of oral tradition, as opposed to the written and printed word. Much of this may seem obvious, especially to the members of ISAC. I apologize if I am telling you something you already know.

Though displaced from the land they celebrated, Southeastern indigenous people had stories, songs and forms of oratory that were once incredibly rich and advanced. This diversity reflected the vast number and density of populations interacting with one another, as well as the region's thriving towns, trading paths, unique waterways and ancient agricultural base. Nowhere else except possibly in California did so varied a pattern of intermingling cultures, did such a mélange emerge, with Creek, Choctaw and other so-called Civilized Tribes, roving Siouan bands, Algonquians from the north, proud neutral states like the Yuchi, and remains of ancient empires (e.g., Calusa, Natchez Indians). Not all of these tribes were 'Indian'. Very ancient European contributions to New World DNA are reflected in the X-gene recently discovered by population geneticists. C. S. Rafinesque in his *Ancient History* long ago proposed Kentucky and Tennessee as the center of an antediluvian Western-style civilization, as evidenced by their numerous mounds, circular stone temples and other monuments. Curtis' *The Indians' Book* (1907) first popularized American Indian oral traditions, creating the earliest anthology of 'oral literature'. But inclusions from Southeastern native people were few and they have continued to be underrepresented.

It is hard for modern-day *readers* to imagine the world of native *speakers*. Word of mouth enjoyed the same primacy as a medium of knowledge, and as a means of religious practice, as do literacy and scripture in Old World religions. Storytelling, chant, song, ceremony, 'talks' and visions were originated and perpetuated by the common people rather than reserved to a privileged few. Religion permeated everything. Orality ensured the communal, continual and egalitarian nature of tribal religions--better termed 'spiritualities'. For Indians, oral tradition is sacrosanct, like the transmission of texts and writings in the West and Orient. If Christianity is book-based, the religions of the Southeast are oral-based. Paper, books and laws were quickly recognized as inimical to indigenous ways. Language itself was taught to people by God (Creek 'Master of Breath'). The second highest rank in any community was the politico-religious dignitary called 'speaker' (Cherokee *skalilosken*), and all towns had criers and greeters, usually wise old men skilled in tribally specific markings and intertribal protocols. The equivalent term for priest or scribe is 'keeper'. Even laws (Adair's 'beloved speech') were oral. There is no theology in Indian society because nothing is written (Deloria). By the same token, there are no lawyers: forensic oratory, so prized in the West, did not develop (Kennedy). History is the story of the people as a whole—men, women and children. It rarely follows the Latin model of deeds of famous men (*res gestae)*. Only occasionally is it a Herodotean collection of times and travels. Never does it approach the Augustinian *City of God* model of philosophical reflection and psychological drama. The past is seen as a place rather than a time. Indeed, most stories are about places — mountains, caves, streams, pools, lakes, cliffs, islands — often as a way of explaining their sacredness.

Among the more unusual productions are autobiographies of a people, oral histories in the first person plural that speak for all Indians. Some modern-day 'speakers' or 'seers' such as Archie Sam (Cherokee-Creek-Natchez Indian, 1914-1986) have been placed on videotape and even broadcast. The intertribal body of knowledge passed to them — seer tradition — can concern past, present or future and pertain to any of three worlds, or dimensions — upper, middle or lower. A prophet (e.g. Josiah Francis, or Hillis Harjo) is thus someone who sees the future, correctly interprets the past or discerns the meaning of current events. Often he is helped by medicine beings such as the Tie-Snakes that appeared from a pool of water to the Tuckabatchee Creeks during Tecumseh's pressuring of them to go to war.

Indian seer tradition tells of the white man's "gold ships," a mercantile empire based in Spain, Canaan and the British Isles that long held sway over the Atlantic coast of North America. The person called Jesus is remembered in some of these traditions as an astute businessman who offended his powerful Davidic family by neglecting his duties and was turned over to Roman authorities. Seer tradition is even so explicit as to say the Vatican possesses records of the historical Jesus in its archives, but they are all rather insignificant commercial accounts and they are now almost destroyed by having been attacked by a fungus. Some of the rules of trade were that no Easterner could remain on Turtle Island (the Americas) over the winter. The traders were content, in turn, if Indians killed chance trespassers. They kept the secret of the Blessed Isles very well—so well, in fact, that the flat earth theory was official until the end of the Middle Ages and most people thought they would fall off the end of the earth if they ventured too far on the surrounding Ocean. The Gold Ships can possibly explain some of the riddles of southeastern epigraphy like the Metcalf stone, Bat Cave and Carthaginian coin hordes in Georgia. These Easterners seem to correspond to Rafinesque's Atalans, white, bearded strangers who had "built above one thousand towns on the waters of the Ohio, of which nearly two hundred were in Kentucky, and the remains of above one hundred are seen to this day. The population must have been as great as the actual one, and Kentucky must have had half a million of inhabitants at least…. The last remains…still existing towards 1500, were the following: —The Wocons in Carolina [Waccamaws], the Homoloas [Timucuas?], Malicas, Apalachians and others in Georgia and Florida, the Conoys of Virginia, the Nanticoes of Maryland, the Catabas of Carolina, the Cahuitas [Koasiti] and Calusas of Alabama, the Tunicas of Louisiana, the Corans, Coras or Escoros of Missouri, Arkanzas, Carolina, California and Mexico; besides many nations of Anahuac [South America]." Both Indian seer tradition and

Rafinesque agree that some settlers of the Americas were white and came from the East, a theory which is supported by the newly discovered "X gene." Significantly, James Adair regarded the Conoys and others in this list as Canaanite tribes.

Rafinesque would be called a diffusionist today, for he also says: "Before the christian [sic] era a casual intercourse was kept up between the two continents. The Phenicians and Gadesiems [people of Cadiz and Gibraltar] traded to America: this continent was known to the maritime nations of West Europe and North-west Africa. The Numidians went there 2000 years ago, as well as the Celts; they frequented Paria [Surinam] and Hayti principally...till the knowledge of America became almost lost or clouded in fables and legends."

The area that is now southwestern Virginia, western North Carolina, eastern Tennessee, southern West Virginia and southeastern Kentucky was once a wilderness known only to Native American tribes such as the Cherokee and Shawnee and to certain crypto-Jewish remnants of Hernando de Soto's explorations in 1540 and Juan Pardo's expeditions in 1567. There is, however, a continuity between the Atalans, the Spanish conquistadors, the Melungeons and the English colony at Jamestown. The link is the so-called Meherrin Indians. Here is a Native American story from seer tradition:

The Moundbuilders were a great civilization from the South and East. They had kings and nobility. Tuscaloosa, who was seven feet tall, was one of them. He fought De Soto at a place called

Mobile. The tall Indian queen De Soto captured at Cofitachique was the daughter of a Moundbuilder king who ruled a large part of middle Georgia. She managed to slip away with one of the Spaniards' black slaves (a Moor). It was a requirement of Moundbuilder society that a noble had to marry a commoner. They went all over the country on their honeymoon. It was a famous love affair. She was called Pirl. Indians still today name their eldest daughter Pirl. That is because she is seen as the family's treasure, its chest of pearls. It's always spelled P-I-R-L. That's the Indian word for "pearl." Pirl and the black man settled down in North Carolina. Their descendants are the Meherrin Indians.

When the first so-called English explorers did arrive, they were an interesting and multiethnic lot. In 1654, Abram Wood, a Sephardic Jew from a large family that settled first in the Carolinas, ventured across the Allegheny Mountains toward the Blue Ridge and discovered a gap into Cherokee territory, also a river (New River). In 1671, a group of five Virginians revisited this same area and claimed it for Britain. No further explorations were made until August 1716 when Governor Alexander Spotswood, a Moroccan Jew, and "several members of his staff left Williamsburg by coach and proceeded to Germania [a fort]... At Germania this party was supplemented by a number of gentlemen [dubbed the Knights of the Golden Horseshoe], their retainers, a company of rangers and four Meherrin Indians...." Their intent was not merely to claim the area for England but to search for silver mines reputed to be have been abandoned by the early Spanish-Portuguese colonists from Santa Elena. Furthermore, Germanna was not settled by ethnic Germans, but rather by Sephardic Jews from Holland and Bohemia specifically recruited by Spotswood for their mining and metallurgical expertise.

So our second argument from Indian traditions proves the influence of Jews, Moors and other Mediterranean peoples on the indigenous people of the Southeast had a very long past and was nothing new. Perhaps even some dim collective memory animated Jews to return to what was once a rich and thickly populated inland empire in the Appalachians. At any rate, the shock of recognition that flew between Jew and Indian was based on long contact and acquaintance.

My third argument comes from the genealogies of chiefs among the Chickasaw, Cherokee, Choctaw, Creek and Seminole. I would love to talk to you about James Adair, who wrote his famous history of the American Indians "by the side of a Chikkasah female, as great a princess as ever lived" and who I believe was himself of Jewish ancestry . . . or James McQueen, who jumped ship as a lad in Pensacola harbor in 1719, married a series of Creek princesses, lived to be 128 years old and was the grandfather of Tecumseh, Osceola and Josiah Francis (Hillis Harjo) . . . or Sequoyah, who came from a Jewish family from Baltimore and married with the Gratz family of Philadelphia and Lancaster. But time forces me to pass them over. Still, I will mention that Montgomery, Alabama was founded by a Jewish trader from Charleston who was forced to marry a Creek Indian chief's daughter whom he had gotten pregnant. Benjamin Hawkins, the Indian agent, referred to him as "Abraham M. Mordecai, a Jew of bad character" (*Letters of Benjamin Hawkins 1796-1806*). Pickens interviewed Mordecai for his history of early Alabama and remarked: "Abram Mordecai, an intelligent Jew, who dwelt fifty years in the Creek Nation, confidently believed that the Indians were originally of his people." Many Indian traders in the Southeast not labeled as such appear to be Sephardic Jewish on the basis of their names. Most of them married a daughter or niece of the relevant Cherokee, Choctaw, Chickasaw or Creek headman. It was common for anyone remaining within the nation over one winter to take a wife and thereby become an adoptive citizen.

Among early Indian traders were Benjamin and James Burges (from the Spanish city of Burgos? — they later changed the name to Burkes and were intermarried with the Coopers), William and Joseph Cooper (a trail guide and linguister active among the Cherokee since 1710, said to be the first ones), Cornelius Dougherty (since 1724 — another family that moved from the Lower Towns to the Upper Towns in Tennessee), Eleazor Wiggans (whose Indian name was Old Rabbit, license revoked 1714, a corroborator of the Jewish descent theory about Indians), James Beamer (from Boehmer, "Bohemian"?), the namesake of the Cherokee headman called Judd's ("Jew's") Friend, John and Daniel Ross, Christian Russel ("a Silician"), Nicolas White ("a native of Mersailles, but resident in this nation 30 years"), Mrs. Durant (a female trader), Obediah Low, John Van, James

Lessle (Lesley), James Lewis, Aron Harad, Zachariah Cox (a land developer), Richard Sparks (a captain at Tellico Blockhouse), Gen. James Robertson (founder of Nashville, Roberson, "of Moro District"), Abraham Gindrat, Davis (a blacksmith), John Marino ("a Spaniard"), John Sheppard, John Clark, McBean, and McKee. Moreover, the trading houses of Clark in Virginia; Rae, Galphin and McGillivray of Augusta; Panton, Leslie, and Company in Pensacola and the Francis family of silversmiths appear to have Sephardic mercantile connections in London, Amsterdam, Barbados and the Barbary Coast.

Let us content ourselves with establishing *when* intermarriage between Jews and Indians became frequent. Apparently, the answer is among the Chickasaws. From the earliest English contact with them, this powerful tribe of Muskogean-speaking Indians that dominated the bluffs on the Mississippi around Memphis was called the Halfbreeds. By 1800, after the area had returned to the Spanish, there was just one town of Halfbreeds left.

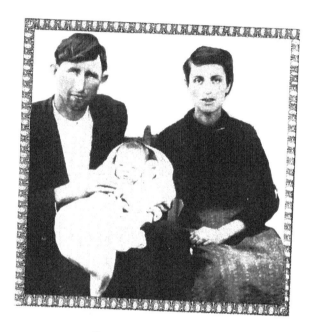

I should have known, since my
grandmother's name was Palestine

8 RETURN TO JUDAISM

"Remarks on Our Return to Judaism," by Donald N. Yates, Mickve Israel, Savannah, Georgia, December 26, 2002

When Rabbi [Arnold Mark Belzer] told me he wanted me to say a few words to you today on the occasion of our return to Judaism, I asked him what I should say. "Just tell them the story," he said. Well, I'm going to do that. I'm going to tell you several stories that explain why my wife Teresa and I both are returning to Judaism, and why it is a return rather than a conversion. But first I'd like to share with you a rather funny little episode.

We couldn't understand why it was funny *then*. It was only after we became "MOT" ["members of the tribe"] that we truly got it. It concerns our first Passover at Arnold and Arlene's. Now maybe I didn't say that right. It was our first

Passover, and it was at Arnold and Arlene's. There were over 80 people in a tent pitched between their back door and pool. We were seated at what might be called the eclectic table. There was a French painter, a stagy black man from New York in a gold kaftan, a Scotsman and a rather uncomfortable looking Old Savannah couple who probably wished they'd sat somewhere else.

Every time a new course would be served, Teresa would say brightly, "Oh, what is this, and what are we supposed to do with it, this is our first Passover!" Everyone just howled at those words "our first Passover." I couldn't understand why. "When are we supposed to drink?" she'd ask. "This is our first Passover." Gales of laughter. "What do the words to that song mean—this is our first Passover."

I didn't figure it out until much later that the reason those words were so funny to the other guests was they could not remember going to their first Passover. They'd been hauled around to Passovers since they were babies. They probably learned to sing "Who Knows One" and how to drink Manischiewitz in the womb.

Well, this is my first time to be called up here, so go easy on me!

How did we find out we were Jewish? All I can say is there were signs. Both my wife and I grew up in northwest Florida in old Southern families that described themselves as English-Scots-Irish, part Cherokee. They were nominally Christian. My wife's mother, a Newberry, made a point of telling her she was named after a little Jewish girl in Arizona. My grandfather, a direct descendant of

Cherokee chief Black Fox, never set foot in a church until they buried him. If that counts.

My grandmother's name was Palestine Cooper, of blessed memory; Teresa's grandmother was Etalka, which we later learned was Yiddish.

Growing up, going to college and graduating and going into the corporate world of business, I always seemed to end up with Jewish friends and associates. My first wife was from a secularized Sephardic Jewish Viennese New Yorker family, so my two children from that marriage—Paul and Alice—have a mother who is Jewish, non-practicing but Jewish nonetheless.

Paul is with us today. He is a financial representative in L.A. Alice is a college student studying economics on her year abroad in Monterey, Mexico. Teresa's two girls, Angela and Kathryn, had a father who, unbeknownst to us all, was Jewish. Angela and Kathryn are also here today from Pensacola, with their children, Seth and Jayden.

As for me, it got so bad that when a new vice president of public relations came on board at the company where I worked—his name was Barry Cohen—he evidently just assumed I was Jewish.

Two months after he started, it was Yom Kippur. "You are a *lantsmann*, aren't you?" he said in disbelief. Well, I was Jewish, only I didn't know it yet.

When I met and married Teresa, I had the uncanny feeling we were related. We were both very much interested in genealogy, and the Internet had just opened up enormous possibilities. We kept running up against a mysterious new ethnic group — the Melungeons.

My Coopers were Melungeon. Teresa's Rameys were Melungeon. My Blevinses were Melungeon. Teresa's Goods were Melungeon. My Sizemores were Melungeon. Teresa's Whiteheads were Melungeon. Every single surname in our family tree was Melungeon, and all the Melungeons were intermarried.

When we plotted our genealogy chart it looked more like a telephone pole than a tree. It only had one branch, and that was the same as the main trunk. Everybody married cousins, it seemed.

There are many theories about the Melungeons — that they were descendants of shipwrecked Portuguese sailors who married Indians, or that they were the descendants of Sir Walter Raleigh's Lost Colony at Roanoke, or that they were a mixture of Moors, blacks and Indians. Only one thing was clear: whatever the Melungeons were, we were virtually line bred.

As I said, we hardly had a non-Melungeon name, and we had our family histories back ten or more generations. So we decided to go visit Teresa's Aunt Elzina in Huntsville, Alabama. Elzina LaVera Grimwood was the keeper of skeletons and reigning matriarch, the daughter and granddaughter of schoolteachers, and the sixth in a series of Tennessee Elzinas that stretched back to the days of Daniel Boone. If anyone could tell us what the big secret was it was Elzina.

Her reply to our questions? (Pause) "You will *never* find out the truth about our people." We both agreed this probably didn't mean that the big secret was that the family had bootleggers, or were

French, or had Indian blood.

Then when Elzina was lying on her deathbed, I received an e-mail from Dr. Elizabeth Hirschman, a marketing professor at Rutgers University, who had just written a book entitled *Melungeons: The Last Lost Tribe in America*. I'll never forget that moment.

It was a real epiphany. The e-mail was captioned simply "Cooper ethnicity?" I knew immediately that Beth, who is also with us here today, was right. The Coopers were Jewish. So were the Rameys, the Goods, the Yateses, the Blevinses and all the others. Beth cut the Gordian knot and showed through DNA analysis that the core Melungeon population consisted of crypto-Jews.

Only when the Ku Klux Klan stirred up the flames of racism in the post-war South did our grandparents and great-grandparents withdraw behind silence and resignation, bury their Jewish heritage entirely and refuse to pass it to the next generation.

They had lost their Indianness or concealed it earlier, though many walked the Trail of Tears all the same. Yes, I am descended from Indian chiefs and rabbis, though the old people might have called us Black Dutch or Black Irish in subterfuge.

And if any of you should wonder why they concealed such a splendid heritage, remember they lived for the most part in the rural Christian South, in small towns. There are instances of Jewish Coopers in Georgia, Alabama, Tennessee and Arkansas who were burned out, lynched, and murdered.

Not long after that fateful e-mail, we began to take our first baby steps toward returning to the fold. One Tuesday afternoon, I took a tour of Mickve Israel with a busload of New Yorkers. "Which one of you is it?" asked Rabbi, meaning which one had suddenly discovered their Judaism. "Both," we said, to his surprise. Next, we screwed up our courage and went to evening services. When it came time for the Shema, a shiver ran through my body. I seemed to recognize the words and melody. We knew we were home. After that service, we broke bread with y'all, including the family sitting in front of us, whose name happened to be Yates, and met the organist, also a Yates.

Rabbi cracked us up by telling everybody once, "There are more Yateses than Cohens here tonight." But seriously, I want to thank this congregation, and Arlene and Arnold especially, for the warm, uncomplicated welcome you have extended to us. We have now completed our first year of Jewish life, celebrating our second Hanukkah, and were immersed at the mickve last Friday.

Next I would like to share with you some reactions from my family members and friends.

My mother: "Well, what of it?"

My oldest brother: "Oh, those are all just names from the Bible."

Our Jewish friend Debi: "I'm going to need therapy after this."

Sis: "I don't want to be Jewish; I want to be an Indian princess."

Mother, some weeks later, to Teresa: "Is Don still going to that new church in Savannah?"

For every negative reaction, though, there were a dozen positive ones. Rabbi Belzer, temple administrator Anne Maner and the others, Cantor Pinkus and Para-Rabbi Julie Hirsch, consistently and instinctively, treated our decision as a return, not a conversion. Every time we went to services, driving in from Statesboro and driving back late at night, often after fellowship with the members of the Shabbat Supper Club, we invariably remarked to each other how lucky we were to have such a wonderful rabbi. He is truly an endless fund of understanding, intelligence and humanity. He sets the tone for what I am proud to think of one of the most enlightened, vital and unified reform congregations in America.

What have I learned over the past year? First of all, I learned that you are never done studying the rich traditions, subtleties and strengths of the Torah and Jewish history. You can never arrive at a point where you can say, "That's enough." There are many similarities here between Judaism and American Indian spirituality.

Both are extremely ancient religions, both have gone through wave after wave of persecution and genocide, both have given big gifts to the world. Before I discovered my Jewish identity, I strove to be a good Indian, a true human being, as they say. The tribal name of the Cherokee in their own language is Ani-Yunwiya ("the real people"). Now I try to be a good Jew. Both religions are what I would call commandment-driven or covenant-driven. Great Spirit does not care so much about what we say as what we do. If we do something wrong, it is sufficient to gain knowledge thereof, ask forgiveness and do it differently.

He has given us his laws to read in the book of nature, he has given us instructions to follow according to our place in the great circle of life. An Indian's Bible is written on the wind, as the Lakota medicine man Matthew King says. A good Indian seeks to walk with a sacred step. Being an Indian is not something you do just one day of the week, in a special place. It is something you live, eat, sleep and dream.

In the same spirit, you cannot be a half Jew or a quarter Jew. You cannot be a Jew once a week or twice a year. I see nothing irreconcilable, nothing incompatible, about Indian spirituality and Judaism. Both systems are earthy, at the same time mystical; both are, in a word, profoundly humanistic. Let there be no mistake, though. I am a Jew in religion. I am an Indian by blood and upbringing. There really is no Indian religion; it is more accurate to call it a culture or spirituality.

In conclusion, I learned Judaism is not a lineage, it's not in the blood, it's not a class, it's not a caste. It's not a political party, it's not a nationality. It's *more* than a culture or tradition. Like being Indian, Judaism is a spiritual path—the one and right path for us. It is a journey more than a destination. In a profound and philosophically paradoxical sense, it is a becoming of what you are.

I finally know at the age of fifty-two what I am and what most of my ancestors have been. If I can leave you with only one thought it is this: We are all Jews by choice…. Our growth in Judaism, our learning, our worshiping together, is a long process of return. We affirm and reaffirm our choice with every step we take along the way. Teresa and I could not be more blessed than to have the family of Mickve Israel as our traveling companions, and we thank you, we honor you all for being there, and we are grateful to you for accepting us back.

Gone Home

9 INDIANS AND CRYPTO-JEWS

"DNA Testing of Southeastern American Indian Families to Confirm Jewish Ethnicity," Paper Delivered by Donald Panther-Yates at the Society for Crypto Judaic Studies Conference, San Antonio, August 3, 2003

The project I will be speaking about today is the first of its kind I am aware of. It grew out of the Melungeon Surname DNA Project started by Beth Hirschman, who was inspired — or manic enough at the time — to spring for the funds.

The project called for volunteers to take either a female descent or male descent genetic test if they could provide reasonable genealogical proof that they were descended either from an early Indian trader or a Native American woman who married or had children with one. The odds were all against us. In order to qualify, the descent of the trader or his wife could not cross from the male to the female line; it had to be either the outside male line, father to son, father to son, or the outside female line, mother-daughter, mother-daughter. We could not, for instance, test one individual who claimed, very eloquently and convincingly, to be descended from both Pocahontas and her sister-cousin Princess Cleopatra. I received a fair measure of hate mail from professors of Indigenous Studies. One volunteer, a Collins in Kentucky, wrote to me about Torah study in her local band of the Saponi, though she assured me they were all good Christians. I also got an interesting letter from the chief of a Tennessee band of the Cherokee who lamented the fact that the tribe members were going through their fourth round of DNA testing without proving much Indian blood. They *had* found so much Jewish types among them that one of them decided to adopt the name "Rolling Bagel."

Some of the test subjects invariably got cold feet and bowed out. I am particularly sorry to have missed the linear descendant of James Adair (author of the first anthropological study of American Indians), the linear descendant of Abraham Mordecai (founder of the town of Montgomery, Alabama), and the linear descendant of Cherokee Chief John Looney (whose ancestors were the famous Luna family of Portugal, among them "the Woman Who Defied Kings"). On the positive side, though, we hit paydirt by locating people with the right credentials and level of cooperation for a number of important historical figures. These included Nancy Ward, the Beloved Woman of the Cherokee Nation, who has more than 12,000 known descendants alive today; Col.

William Holland Thomas, the Welsh trader who founded the Eastern Band of Cherokee Indians in North Carolina; Chief John Bowles, the leader of the Texas Band of Cherokees; and Elizabeth Tassell, said to be the first Cherokee to marry a white man, (Ludovic Grant, a Scottish trader). To these may be added an ancestor both Beth and I have in common — William Cooper, an explorer and trader who was the scout for Daniel Boone.

What I'm going to do is run through the numbers first, then talk about a few of the genetic types on both the female (mostly Indian) side and white (mostly male) side, then sum up with some observations about the early mixing of Indians and Jews in the Colonial period. You will see that admixture between Jews and Indians is a sort of Eastern parallel to the experiences you are probably more familiar with in the American Southwest. I've brought all my files with my on a laptop if anyone is interested in seeing specific data or is curious about pursuing a connection after the lecture.

First, the numbers. There were 9 persons, mostly females, who took the Native Match test, and 12 persons, necessarily males, who took the Y chromosome test. Only one test result came back Unknown. Many of the haplotypes were unique, meaning they matched no sample in either Bennett's clientele at Family Tree DNA or the larger databases he cross-indexes to, including Michael Hammer's. This shouldn't surprise us because the DNA testing of Native Americans has been very limited, controversial, concentrated in any event on Navajos and other Western reservation tribes. Peter Jones of the Bäuu Institute in Boulder, Colorado, recently published an important paper criticizing the whole state of anthropological genetics and calling for an entirely new beginning. Of the five lineages the current state of scholarship classifies as Native American — haplogroups A, B, C, D and X — our project found 2 Cs and one B, no A, no D, and one X, the latter in an uncle of one of our participants. The majority of those hoping to authenticate their female Indian ancestry (5 out of 9) proved to be H, the most common European haplogroup. One was J, the classic Jewish/Semitic haplogroup. As for the Y chromosome haplogroups, half (6 out of 12) were R1b (sometimes called the Atlantic Modal Haplogroup), 2 (17%) were E3b, one of two well-studied Jewish haplogroups, and one was J2, the second well-established type. There were also single entries in the categories of Viking (Locklear, a Lumbee Indian name), Native American (Sizemore), and as I mentioned, one sample that turned out to be a "big unknown."

So those are the results we are dealing with. Both Beth and I — I'm not sure about Bennett — were impressed with the fact that, though this was just a small sample, it produced the same proportion of what we might call male Jewish DNA, roughly 20 percent, vis à vis 80 percent male non-Jewish DNA, as is the proportion in most studies of both Sephardic and Ashkenazi populations. On the female side, the most startling result was a strong hint that there were females carrying Middle Eastern genes among the Cherokees even before so-called "white contact" in the eighteenth century.

For our first break-out, let's talk about the results for a woman whom I shall Jasmine, for she showed the J haplogroup in her female line. Jasmine was very forthcoming with documentation, names, dates and a lot of family history that would probably not have been shared and made available under other circumstances. She claimed strict matrilineal descent from Betsy Walker Hyde, a native girl born about 1718, who was captured in a military attack by the English and raised by Sen. Felix Walker. Her descendant, Catherine Hyde, was remembered as a "full blood Cherokee." Catherine became the mistress of Col. Will Thomas and bore him several children. Jasmine put me in touch with the last, lone descendant of one of Col. Will's other daughters, whom he fathered with another native woman, Demarius Angeline Thomas Sherril. The mtDNA there was haplogroup X, a rare Native American lineage which may have come from Europe or the Middle East, not Asia. There are many reasons to think Col. Thomas himself was a crypto-Jew. His mother was a Calvert, and the Holland surname is often associated with Jews from the Netherlands. Supporting the suspicion these people were crypto-Jewish culture are the names they gave their children: Demarius (Tamar), Darthelia, Joshua, Parmelia and (my favorite) Docie Beatrice.

Let us go now to the man who turned out to bear Jewish male DNA. I was extremely pleased to get correspondence from the descendants of Col. John Bowles, the founder of the Texas Band of the Cherokee. Chief Bowles died leading a war party, shot in the back by a white man near Redlands,

Texas, in 1839. We located two elderly brothers in Oklahoma who were great-great-great grandsons of the legendary chief. To everyone's surprise Bowles DNA came back J2, with a two-step mutation matching a person identified as Ashkenazi from the Ukraine. How could this be? Bowles was similar to other Cherokee chiefs of his day in being a halfbreed. His father was a Scottish trader and his mother a full-blood Cherokee. When his father was killed and robbed by two North Carolinians in 1768, John was only twelve years old, but within two years the fair-complexioned, auburn haired boy had killed both his father's slayers. After that, he became a Chickamauga warrior. He was called The Bowl (in Cherokee, Duwali). And he was not the only "white chief." Another during the same period was The Glass, whose name in the North Carolina settlements was originally Thomas Glass. Chief Black Fox, my ancestor was a Scotsman descended from Blacks and Foxes. I believe all these families were Scottish crypto-Jews. They were heavily intermarried, generation after generation.

I ran a search for matches on Bowles DNA in the Y-STR Haplotype Reference Database. There were 17 matches in Europe—Albania, Berlin, Budapest, Bulgaria, Bydgoszcz in northern Poland, Cologne, Colombia (2), Freiburg, Latium, Pomerania, Stuttgart, Sweden, Tyrol, Umbria, Warsaw and Westphaia. A "one-off" mutation produced Freiburg and Lombardy. The picture that emerged was one that closely echoed the distribution pattern for the Gothic invasions that repeopled Italy, France and Spain. To the contrary, the predominant matches in our Melungeon surname study have led to the Iberian Peninsula and to places like Antioquia, Colombia, where Marranos and crypto-Jews emigrated. Here was a Jewish haplotype that, historically speaking, seemed to have traveled out of Scandinavia and the Baltic region, passed through Italy to Spain and Scotland and migrated on to the Americas, where it mingled with the Indians.

In another of our surnames, Rogers, one can also trace the footsteps of the Goths.

How about Wales as an unlikely place to find Jews? Our project established the Jewish origins of another great pioneer family of the South who intermarried with Cherokees, the Blevinses. Two of our Blevins test subjects were found to have E3b genes, which even Bennett admits are Ashkenazic. The name Blevins originates in Britain and by the seventeenth century was associated with the little port town of Formby. It may be derived from *(a)b* (Welsh for "son of") and Levin (meaning Levite). William Blevins, born in Rhode Island, was a Long Hunter who explored Kentucky and Tennessee with Elisha Wallen in 1734. His son had two Cherokee wives, sisters, and a multitude of Blevinses appear on the Cherokee rolls. All are my cousins, as my great-great-grandmother was Mahala Jane Blevins. The Blevins family has occasionally shown itself to be openly Jewish. Bertha Blevins, a declared Jewess, married Moses H. Cone, who was born in Jonesboro, Tennessee, in 1857. She endowed the Greensboro (N.C.) Health Care System upon her death in 1947.

Now it is time to look at the American Indian

results. We were fortunate in being able to sample the DNA of two key female figures in Cherokee history. Elizabeth Tassell (we might as well call her a "princess" as long as the American Indian Movement or sticklers in the BIA are not listening), married Ludovic Grant, a Scottish trader about 1720. His name probably comes from French *Grand*, German *Gross*. The couple's descendants are the oldest of the bloodlines studied in a definitive fashion by Emmett Starr, whose genealogies were the basis for government blood quantums and tribal membership. One of Elizabeth Grant's eleventh-generation descendants, with a long Dutch name, joined our study and her DNA proved to be haplogroup C. This was also the haplogroup of an Oklahoma descendant of Nancy Ward, the famous Beloved Woman. Both participants preserve their clan affiliation, which is Wolf Clan.

Does this tell us anything? I think it does. One's clan was passed from the mother to her children in a strict matrilineal fashion, just like mitochondrial DNA.

Another test subject, a San Francisco man, matched a woman of Hispanic descent with a crypto-Jewish surname. He carried B lineage and the family still preserved the fact they were Long Hair Clan.

Haplogroup C, notably, has a large "cline" in the southern Appalachians. The B haplogroup, concentrated in the Southwest, appears to fit the Pueblo Indians.

Let me mention a "Big Unknown," before concluding. This was an 80-year-old gentleman in

California by the Scottish-sounding name of McAbee who generously joined our study, with the help of his niece. Their family had a sturdy tradition of crypto-Jewish practices in Kentucky, including opening the door for the prophet Elijah on special days. Everybody drew a blank over his DNA, which was finally classified as "Unknown." It was described by all the rest of us as "eerie." The family claimed they were descended from Judas Macabbaeus. Could it be true? As I learned, it is indeed a very rare haplotype. The closest matches in the Y-user database in Berlin were in Albania, Bulgaria/Romani, London and with a Bulgarian Turk. If surviving descendants of the Hasmonean Jews, the first convert population, lived anywhere it would likely be in those places.

The last DNA test results I would like to talk about were those of a verifiable crypto-Jewish family among the Choctaw and Chickasaw Indians. This was a male paternal-line descendant of Louis LeFleur/LeFlore, a French Canadian trader who married Rebecca Cravat, said to be an "Indian princess." He introduced the first cattle, hogs, keel boats, cotton and tobacco crops to the Choctaw. LeFlore thus occupies the same position of Culture Bearer as Nancy Ward holds among the Cherokee. His son Greenwood became the principal chief of the Choctaw, married a Jewish Cherokee woman named Elizabeth Coody and managed to stay in Mississippi after Indian removal. One branch of the family in modern times changed its name to Flores, which seems to be the original Portuguese form. Flores is a big Marrano surname. A run through the Y-STR database confirmed numerous Iberian and

Latin American matches, with Asturias and Central East Spain being the strongest hits.

One of the really cool things about DNA analysis is finding a match and making contact with people you would never have dreamed you are related to. When we got the results for Gayle Wilson, an enrolled Cherokee in Oklahoma, and found out she carried the Nancy Ward gene, a young schoolteacher in California by the name of Juan Madrid wrote to us inquiring how he could have matched her. Madrid, of course, is a fairly common Marrano name. But he had no tradition of being Cherokee. His grandmother lived among the Comanches, and all the family would talk about is "some Indian blood somewhere," without being specific. Juan definitely had the Cherokee Wolf Clan gene, and he is now pursuing tribal enrollment. I found out he already had an Indian name. Significantly, he is called Two Hearts.

It is time to draw some conclusions and end. Bennett has repeatedly assured both Beth and me that there is no such thing as "Jewish DNA." Strictly speaking, it's true. There are haplogroups into which the DNA of people known to be Jewish today fall. But even some Arabs and Muslims test positive for the Cohen gene. So how can we be so sure the Y chromosomal haplotypes we are studying are Jewish? The answer lies in a chain of circumstantial evidence. The overwhelming preponderance of surnames with Hebrew and Sephardic Jewish roots, combined with multigenerational cousin marriage and other historical factors, cannot be ignored. Genetics without a good genealogical chart is useless. Even the charts can sometimes be misleading unless one has access to death-bed confessions and whispered family traditions.

Only in the last two years did I find out my family was Jewish, or perhaps better said, crypto-Jewish. There is not a single surname in my family tree, which I have traced back more than 700 years in some lines, that defies the pattern. Despite all this, though, I always wanted to find something concrete and unequivocal, something of the vanished past I could touch with my hands and cling to in my thoughts. So this spring I made a pilgrimage to New Hope Cemetery on Sand Mountain in Tennessee where my great-great-great grandmother Mahala Jane Blevins Cooper is said to be buried.

New Hope is a beautiful, forgotten place. The dogwoods and redbuds were in flower; it was Sunday morning. The Cooper-Blevins burial plot was on the edge of the cemetery with the oldest stones, rough unmarked header and footer rocks, unlike the rest of the graves. I took a picture of my great-uncle Harmon Cooper's memorial. It had the Freemason or Templar cross and showed a hand pointing to the sky, with the words GONE HOME. I was thrilled, satisfied at last I had concrete proof, for I'd seen similar designs in the crypto-Jewish burials at Purrysburgh, South Carolina. I cleaned the graves … put down a tobacco offering in the Indian manner … said the Shema and Shecheyanu … and wished I had learned the Mourner's Kaddish. I finally experienced what I think I had been looking for all along … a strong feeling that the ancestors were placated and pleased. If I have accomplished nothing else, I would like to leave you with this. We all have a moral imperative to uncover our families' past. They would have been proud of us.

ANCESTORS AND ENEMIES

Ruck Sizemore
The Last Chickamauga Medicine Man

10 CYBERFEUD ON THE RIDGE

Oil yore rifle-guns, get yore good glasses on and let out the hounds, because the genealogy wars have erupted and the Melungeons are coming. It's Newman's Ridge against a passel of flatlanders and city slickers in a hair-pulling, rip-snorting fracas that offends against nearly every precept of civil behavior, and most rules of logic and spelling. Anything goes in this jolly tale of "Let's you and him fight."

People agree it was the National Genealogy Society in Washington that fired the first shot. In June 1996, this lily-white, normally harmless body led by members of the Daughters of the American Revolution published a review of Brent Kennedy's book *The Melungeons* in their quarterly magazine. The author was Virginia Easley DeMarce, Ph.D., past president, genealogy hobbyist and science fiction writer, who worked for the Office of Federal

Acknowledgment, Bureau of Indian Affairs, U.S. Department of the Interior.

"Mercer University Press has placed its imprimatur on a book that attempts to cross the disciplines of anthropology, genealogy, and history with genetics as a periodic refrain," Dr. DeMarce began her attack. "However, the author does not apply the standard methodology of any of these disciplines. Racial prejudice and persecution, as the title implies, are the themes that meld all this together. A chronological leap over several centuries enables the author to propose an exotic ancestry for "200,000 individuals, perhaps far more" (p. xv) — an ancestry that sweeps in virtually every olive, ruddy, and brown-tinged ethnicity known or alleged to have appeared anywhere in the pre-Civil War Southeastern United States."

The keepers of the sacred national character were clearly alarmed at the prospect of hundreds of thousands of "olive, ruddy, and brown-tinged" individuals reverting to type and demanding the equal treatment that history and custom had denied them. Mindful of the unpleasant civil rights agitation of the Sixties and Seventies and uncomfortable memories dredged up by the Indian Self-Recognition movement, DeMarce took a page from the official playbook of her employer and launched an end-run on this new threat to the Revised Standard Version of America. The "Melungeons" were all proved, by modern science and scrutiny of public records, which are color-blind, to be, if not white, at least just as good as white. Such persons had never been discriminated against. Nothing had been taken away from them, so nothing needed to be restored to them. They had no rights beyond what all the rest of us had. They deserved no special treatment in the history books. Case closed.

Sensing a slight, but not realizing what had run him over, Brent Kennedy promulgated a "response" posted on the Melungeon Heritage Association's website, after more than a year of confusion and defensive manoeuvers. "Of course," he demurred, "much of this back-and-forth bantering could have been avoided if the *National Genealogical Quarterly* had permitted me some sort of response to her 1996 book review. But the editors did not, and the rest as they say, is history." Kennedy gallantly thanked "those journals and websites which did publish my rebuttal" and even went so far as to say he was "generally pleased to see what appears to be Dr. DeMarce's increasing acceptance of a broader-based Mediterranean gene pool for our Appalachian ancestors." But aunts are not gentlemen, as Bertie Wooster was fond of remarking. The damage was done. Kennedy would fight a losing battle against his detractors until he fell from a stroke and his own health forced him into retirement.

Kennedy singled out three key elements in DeMarce's ambush:

> (1) She sees no rationale or evidence for any theorized Turkish infusion, and

> (2) She believes that Melungeons have always been—and remain—a very few isolated families, and that I have broadened the definition of Melungeon to the point of meaninglessness, and

(3) She sees absolutely no evidence that I
personally am of Melungeon descent.

Like a Shakespearean hero, he poured a waste
of spirit in an expense of shame into "responding"
to these three points over the next five years,
without realizing that the grounds of the argument
and rules of engagement were against him. With
the waters muddied, and the hidden hand of
racism and denial sporting free, the term
"Melungeon" is still undefined, fifteen years later.

Things started out peaceably on the new
GenForum Melungeon Forum in June 2000.
Several listers announced they were Melungeon
and proud of it. Then certain members began to
take sides and sow dissension. More than 20,000
posts were to fly from the fingers of subscribers in
one year alone. Under the ominous rubric,
"Irresponsible, self-appointed judges," we find
Perry Spencer posting on July 13, 2000:

> These "notices" are filling this Forum with
> junk and ruining it. I don't want to ignore the
> Williamson messages—or Denham's, either, if
> they have thoughtful content. I do want to
> ignore the goofy, boring, repetititive, childish,
> schizoid drivel.

A user named CDenham felt compelled to
clarify, "Please, fellow posters, be aware that there
are more than one DENHAM on this board. And
all we have in common is the name."

L. Denham shot back: "Well, now aint you
special! Guess that proves that all Denham's dont
use good judgement when they marry! Hope your
children, if any, act more like the Denham's than
whatever line you came from." To which, Perry

Spencer riposted, "Looks and sounds as if the poster has been drinking." It is not known how Perry Spencer could detect the smell of alcohol over the Internet.

On July 12, 2000, the unwelcome Steve Williamson posted, "The whole thing started when I posted the names of the articles by DeMarce & the book by Elder on the Melungeon Forum. Nancy Morrison & Mike Nassau jumped all over me for posting those names, and things just got worse from there. Nancy still has a grudge against me from last year . . . There's a handful of people who are dead sure that Kennedy's theories are the only right ones . . . Those people want to make the forum into their own little private club . . . ."

Next came an admonition from Aaron Aardvark: "Please do not respond to any post by Steve Williamson . . . Do not dignify his rantings by a response." And from Joe Showalter: "Steve Williamson is on official ignore from the responsible members of this forum." This did not prevent Steve Williamson from starting a thread, "For new people who have an open mind." Mike Nassau, again, warned listers that Steve Williamson was "disruptive and insulting," and no one should respond to his posts. Digging into the prelude to this banishment, we find threads with titles like "Diabolical undesirable Anti-Melungeon" and "Blocking undesirables from your site." Delving deeper, we uncover "Steve The Troublemaker," "Sorry, but I had to," "Racist," and "The niceties of civilized discourse."

As would frequently happen in misfortunes overtaking the list, many of the posts leading up to the unmasking of the troublemaker were subsequently removed. It is hard in retrospect to reconstruct many of the threads. When things would calm down, the wreckage left by saboteurs and the cleanup crew would show a scene of puzzling awe and mystery, as when a storm leaves standing the kitchen of a home while carrying off all the other rooms, or a trail of destruction has made a pious detour around a church.

The year 2002 saw Kennedy receive reinforcements for his "theory" from academicians Elizabeth Hirschman of Rutgers and Donald Yates (one of the authors of this book). A Kingsport native, Hirschman was just beginning to build her fame as an expert in Appalachian cultural identity and ethnic consumer behavior after discovering her parents had lied to her about the family's Melungeon ancestry, telling her she was white, Christian and privileged—an ordinary WASP. She, like Yates, had spent the first fifty years of her life under the happy illusion of a false ancestry. A confederate, Donna Snelling, was so taken with their work that she started a thread, "Sephardim DNA Studies," in June.

"Thanks, Donalyn," wrote Sheila Hill of East Tennessee, "this list needed to have factual data on this most important study. I have had the pleasure of conversing with Donald Panther-Yates, and I applaud and respect his efforts. We should all consider that persons such as Dr. Panther-Yates have contributed towards our overall knowledge of multiethnic peoples in the southeast."

But the reaction of most listers was not so receptive. In the thread, "Why the controversy,"

Joanne Pezzullo shot down Donalyn's statement, "The roots of the Melungeons come from an area from PA to FL and way beyond; not all went to or stayed in TN." Pezzullo began to recruit a "Ridge-only" party, while holding to the nihilist school of DeMarce that claimed her Gibsons and others were just plain folks, certainly not Jewish. Ramona Bayes Woods wrote on June 7, "For the life of me I cannot understand why some fellow researchers found her messages regarding Dr. Yates' work on the Sephardim Jews upsetting." But the list owner Dennis Maggard assured everyone, "I have reviewed these Sephardim postings with some care now and see no evidence of anyone on this list being upset about anything." At any rate, the list was purged of discordant messages and again sanitized.

Then came Fourth Melungeon Union, held June 20-22, 2002 in Kingsport, Tennessee. Kennedy, popular and in his prime, welcomed newcomers, rallied the troops and calmed the various factions in a celebration that took place, for the first and last time, literally, in a big tent, one erected for the occasion in a city park. Elizabeth Hirschman presented her DNA findings, and Donald Yates spoke about tie-ins with Southeastern Indians. Nancy Morrison organized a health caucus.

The aftermath of Fourth Union witnessed an irreparable splintering of the movement into hostile camps, now armed with the weapons of modern science. The Melungeon Heritage Society in Wise, Virginia, which had begun to keep a proud Melungeon Registry, was soon wrecked over ideological issues. Bets were all off for any partnership with a university or other sponsoring entity.

As many had rejected the notion of Melungeons being a separate ethnic entity in the first place, so now many refused to believe there was such a thing as Melungeon diseases, especially, it seemed, if Melungeon health sometimes overlapped with well-known Jewish diseases (such as familial Mediterranean fever). A rancorous rift opened up over this issue. "While many of my relatives have been diagnosed with FIBRO, CFS and LUPUS I would like to see this gene traced back to surnames and not a group of people, who in my opinion, were so called FAIRY TALE," Joanne Pezzullo wrote witheringly to Nancy Morrison, on July 6. Nancy reloaded and barraged Joanne with more facts in a thread called "Book OUTDATED by DNA." She would soon be kicked off the list for telling "the story in the hopes of helping others."

By the end of 2002, the deteriorating situation called for a new statement from Kennedy, who once again attempted to be the peacemaker. He zeroed in on five issues. These were: 1) how do I define Melungeon, 2) are there Melungeon diseases, 3) what will DNA studies show, 4) are there "Melungeon" anthropological traits and 5) what is the Melungeon Movement. The battlelines were drawn, obviously, but the defensive nature of the leader's remarks could hardly go unnoticed. The word Melungeon now needed apologetic quotation marks around it.

Trouble continued to brew for those who espoused the Jewish roots of the Melungeons.

Things came to a head in a thread titled "Lord have Mercy," igniting several hundred posts in February of 2003. At the epicenter, Elizabeth Hirschman wrote:

Hi guys, And I thought the folks living here in New Jersey were rough! You folks have got to stop fighting with each other; what a contentious website! To me however, with my 'we're really all Jewish' theory you are just proving my point. The ONLY other place I have ever witnessed such bickering and nitpicking is when I attended a Jewish Conference two years ago where they were discussing who was and was not a Jew. Oddly enough, that discussion/fight almost exactly paralleled the issues on this board. BUT, just like here, it only hurt peoples' feelings and got us nowhere in terms of creating group cohesion or intellectual progress. In two years or so, the present discussion won't be relevant, because by then a LARGE set of DNA scores will be available for many families in the region. What we are going to learn (and already are learning) is that virtually all of the families have Iberian-Jewish ancestry, plus some Arab, some Turkish, some Berber, some Native American and some African American in given lines. DNA-wise, physically, and ethnically we are going to be pretty much indistinguishable from one another regardless of whether we come from Tennessee, Virginia, North Carolina, Kentucky, West Virginia, Arkansas, Missouri or Texas—because these are the places our ancestors migrated and kept

intermarrying and intermarrying ad infinitum.
Adios and shalom, Beth

A rift developed between Pat Elder, a
Melungeon author, and Brent Kennedy. In the
same thread, Kelly Pritchard told Pat, "Time for a
big time out & go sit in a corner." Pat had written
(February 10, 2002), "Have you ever seen anyone as
arrogant as Kennedy? I am wondering why he
decided to attack Malinda Yates? He was pretty
nasty to her I thought."

Malinda Yates hastened to stipulate (March 2,
2003): "Hi, Melungeon Movement. I have been
keeping abreast of the happenings on this list from
the archives and yes I am a real person, but have
only signed back on this list to emphatically state *I
am not* realted (sic) to Donald Panther Yates as
some have claimed in a private email to me. Thank
you very much, Malinda."

Kelly Pritchard further told Pat Elder:

Just think for the rest of history of this list,
people researching you and putting your name
in a simple search engine like Google will be
treated to a copy of your personal attack on
Brent Kennedy. Is that your intentions? Not
very honorable, nor nice. Now go sit in the
corner for 15 minutes while repeating to
yourself, "If I can't say anything nice, I will say
it off list. " Spare us, please. I thank you in
advance for future use of good manners.

Judy Lang weighed in with:

Yes, Pat. I think you are more arrogant
than Kennedy, but you are also rude and you
demean your fellow list members. You are so
quick to draw the first blood with sarcasm,

and then turn around and say somebody else was being nasty. This has been a pattern of yours lately. I hope you will not wake up tomorrow and regret so much of what you are saying today, as you did last time, unless that regret catalizes a change.

But Joanne Pezzullo had the last word:

Let he who is without sin cast the first stone. Pat apologized, Brent accepted, Dennis closed the discussion.

By June, the in-crowd had settled down and seemed in the mood to just have some fun again, meeting on the Cherokee Indian Reservation to play Indians. Penny Ferguson wrote to the Ridge-Only group, "Does anyone have a favorite place they like to stay overnight in Cherokee NC. AND Yates and Hirschmans Melungeon project is to silly to discuss." Her "Silly" thread drew over thirty me-too's.

On June 24, Helen Campbell, who had started a website at Melungeons.com and posted a list of surnames for DNA volunteers, wrote to Joanne Pezzullo:

Joanne, Believe it or not, but there is another world outside of this list... a world that you can not control by your intimidation towards others. Melungeon hugs, Helen

Joanne took aim and wrote back:

Helen this is not about intimidation nor (sic) control. The surnames on that list are not Melungeons. If Hirchman (sic) and Yates wants (sic) to call them Melungeons without any documentation then they should expect people to challenge it.

She wondered why the authors of the Melungeon DNA study hadn't gotten authorization from her. To which Helen replied, "They need no authorization from you." Joanne then retaliated with:

Check the census records helen most of those names are not even found in Virginia or Tennessee. They may not need authorization from anyone but I do not need authorization from anyone to flat out say those are NOT Melungeons in that study . . . If you are talking about the Hirchman-Yates (sic) project they need to rename that Appalachian Study ---- those are not Melungeons.

To a call for volunteers, Suze Griffith wrote on June 25, "I have utterly no problem about going 'public.' I have never tried to hide my heritage. I just want to be sure I'm one of the folks the group is looking for." Betty the Windchaser replied, "Same here. If my Bowling/Bolen line could be established i would be willing to do. And have no problem with being public." She thoughtfully appended the toll-free number for the National Domestic Violence Hotline.

In July, it was time for Penny Ferguson to post, "Would someone please call in a psychiatrist." The subject now was Jack Goins' DNA. Jack had written previously about "Grandpa's Indians" and thought he knew who they were. Elizabeth Hirschman explained to him:

Because Don Panther-Yates and Brent Kennedy also have Native American Sizemore ancestry (although NOT in their direct male-to-male paternal lineage), they are your genetic cousins. They are therefore as "Melungeon" as your Goins are. And indeed the Native American Sizemores have as good a claim to Melungeonness as you do. Beth

Listers got into a shouting match about Nancy Morrison, Helen Campbell and Donald Yates' suggestion that the word Melungeon might have something to do with Angolan Malungu, a part-black mixed group in Brazil. Jack Goins bullied Helen with: "Donald Panther Yates don't believe in documentation" (December 10, 2003). And Janet Crain demanded, "Is Donald Panther-Yates retracting the statement?" (December 30, 2003).

About this time, the Sizemore name came periodically into the crosshairs of the debunkers. Joy King indignantly denied that Sizemores were Native American or Melungeon. Brian Hall just as forcefully claimed they were both, and in fact Jewish to boot. When he announced that he was publishing a book on his Sizemores, the response from others was generally enthusiastic, accepting of the family's Jewish roots. Vicki Swift Landis, for instance, wrote him:

> I am very interested in your book . . . My sisemore ggrand mother marride a cowan and I find they are jewish back ground also. I noticced mis king states there is no proff to the jewisness of sisemores. I would very much like to know if I have jew in me.

But others were less than enthralled. "I'd like to suggest you (and Donald Panther Yates) *personally* do some actual *Sizemore research*," taunted Joy King in rebuttal to Brian Hall's "Sizemore Sephardic Jews" thread on Ancestry.com

(November 23, 2003). "There is *nothing* that would indicate the Richard & John of the 1638 list of Barbados were anything but English." Bonnie sniped: "I wouldn't buy your book" and dismissed Jewishness by pointing out that the Sizemore male line was testing out to be Q or Native American, "just so you know."

Michele went even further, threatening legal action:

> I wonder is Brian and Don Panther Yates (sic) are prepared for a serious lawsuit if any of my Ancestors are mentioned. I fully intend to bring it into a court of law unless every single bit of information is documented. If it isn't, there BETTER be a notation directly visable in that book that says this is just ONE THEORY and not proven beyond a reasonable doubt (April 18, 2004).

Strident capital letters and venom-dipped asterisks ran riot after a Salt Lake City Mormon researcher named Alan Lerwick released the results of his long study of the Sizemores in England. He tied them to the Jewish sector of the city and traced them back to a Michael Sisemor. After some less than friendly back-and-forth with Joy King on the Sizemore message board, Lerwick posted:

> Get off the head trip. That the Sizemore blood is Native American. The male line of Sizemore is Jewish. The earliest record that I have seen of these Sizemores is of a Samuel Sizemore b.abt 1673 that was living in Norfolk, Norfolk Co, VA in 1693. Samuel is likely a brother of William Sizemore b.abt 1675; d.abt 1755 Halifax Co, VA that was living in circa

1712 in Henrico co, VA. William is my
ancestor. William is grandfather of Old Ned
"Edward Sizemore" that married Elizabeth
Rachel Jackson. My line is thru William's son
Ephraim and then thru his son George
Sizemore that died abt 1790 Stokes Co, NC.
(July 9, 2004)

King would become the bête noire of Sizemore
message boards, never giving up on their being
English and non-Jewish. She bedeviled Lerwick
and others for years, condemning any study,
project or testing company that found Jewish
ancestry in Melungeons. Starting her own Sizemore
DNA Surname Project, she clung to the explanation
that Sizemore was an English name. As for the
Sizemore Q lineage, that *could* be a rare
European form of Q, not American Indian.

Donald Yates blogged later on another site that
Sizemore/Sisemor turns out to be traceable to the
Seasmer family, from Hertfordshire, as proven by
English records. A supporting comment from the
user Zoltan pointed out that Csizmár was a well-
known Hungarian surname, from the Turkish
word *csizma* for "boot." Real Jews of the very same
Central European surname were buried in Israel
and listed in the Holocaust Database.

After the original Melungeon Surname DNA
Project on Family Tree DNA began to infer Jewish
roots in many of the participants' male lines, Jack
Goins and several others founded their own study
with the same name, through the same company.
The original Hirschman-Yates project was yanked,
leaving the rival study in sole possession of the
field. In a statement given on February 23, 2010,

Elizabeth Hirschman, the founder of the original project, looked back on these years when many had not wanted to accept there were Jews in Melungeonland:

> Initially, many people in the genetic genealogy community were frustrated that the incoming Jewish DNA results were not originating in the Middle East, as they had strongly believed and hoped (some as Zionists), but were showing a lot of Khazar, Central Asian, Eastern European and Western European/Spanish/French input. Don Panther-Yates and I—and also Ellen Levy Koffman on the DNA-Genealogy list at Rootsweb—had been saying this was the case. Critics were not happy that the data were confirming it.

> Where Don and I have performed a service, I believe, is by just following the DNA trail and accepting new findings (e.g., the Gypsy/Roma) when they come in, instead of clinging to an *a priori* theory/belief/wish. To cite one different approach, a lot of Behar's early 2000s studies now are being criticized for his over-claiming a Middle Eastern origin for the majority of Jews.

Polarization between the various factions went into high gear on the eve of Hirschman's presentation at the El Paso Conference on Crypto-Judaic Studies in August 2006. The Ridgers were in now in lockstep with Bennett Greenspan and other self-appointed arbiters of Jewish genetics. Joanne Pezzullo issued the statement, "For the record Hirschman and Yates 'Melungeons' are not the same as the Melungeons who have been documented to be have had ties (sic) to Newman's Ridge." Nancy Morrison screamed, in all-caps, "IS A MATTER OF OPINION NOT A FACT." Not to be outdone, Pezzullo blasted back, sticking in asterisks and peppering the enemy with a hail of quote marks for effect:

> It is my OPINION the Yates and Hirschman Melungeon DNA project is a joke. It is a FACT 'their Melungeons' are not the same as the Melungeons who have been documented to be have had ties to Newman's Ridge. It apparently is also your OPINION those names are not associated with Melungeons since I checked the names on genforum and you HAVE NOT posted your --- "families living in the area of NC/VA/KY/TN/WV in the last 200+ years *may* belong to a very interesting group of people called MELUNGEONS" and MAY have health issues---- post to few, if any, of them.

Many listers took cover after the gunfights of 2006. Kennedy, Hirschman, Yates, Campbell, Morrison and other proponents of what may be called the Crypto-Jewish hypothesis left the list. When Hirschman and Yates published "Suddenly Melungeon: Reconstructing Consumer Identity across the Color Line," in the technical journal *Consumer Culture Theory* in 2007, the new management of Melungeon-L under Janet Crain as moderator posted a "Word of Caution." Jack Goins wrote on January 10, 2008 ("Confession"):

> Hello list members I must confess, I loved to argue, debate, etc, bla, bla on this list, but

presently I don't have time to post or assist others in their family or Melungeon research. If it does not violate any rules I hereby give Beth permission to use those emails where she accused me of being disingenuous and eventually apologized to the list. I also request her or Donald Panther Yates to explain, confirm how they decided there was a female Melungeon mtDNA test, and also identify that sweet little Melungeon lady who they surely must have used to establish such a test.

Unfortunately, neither Hirschman nor Yates ever heard this humble confession. No one was there to explain to Jack that mitochondrial DNA did not need a "sweet little Melungeon lady," since it was carried by both males and females, and a test to see if your mitochondrial DNA matched other Melungeons might be taken by either a lad or a lady.

Later in the year, Roberta Estes published her long online article "Revealing American Indian and Minority Heritage using Y-line, Mitochondrial, Autosomal and X Chromosomal Testing Data Combined with Pedigree Analysis Revealing American Indian and Minority Heritage using Y-line, Mitochondrial, Autosomal and X Chromosomal Testing Data Combined with Pedigree Analysis." A few years before, like Goins, Sizemore and others, she had decided if you can't lick 'em, join 'em, and started her own DNA consulting business. Invidious comparisons were bound to be made with Donald Yates and the company he had founded in 2003, named DNA Consultants. Estes was duly plugged on the list,

ANCESTORS AND ENEMIES

and when followers of DNA Consultants objected, listers were told by Janet Crain, "Just a reminder that it has been customary to allow a one time courtesy announcement by list members of their website, books, etc. Donald Yates is not a member of this list. Thank You."

Joanne Pezzullo now complained to Janet Crain:

> Janet, With all due respect the article you posted by Roberta Estes in my opinion has nothing to do with Melungeons in the first place. Then you post a link to her 'website' where we can order thousands of dollars worth of tests and analysis and now you say 'you might get lucky'?
>
> As Roberta Estes is part of Family Tree DNA I find this posting as nothing more than an advertisement for Family Tree DNA and the company DNA Explain owned and operated by Roberta Estes. If the results of a DNA test is that hard to understand that one needs to pay hundreds and hundreds of dollars to have someone explain it to them shouldn't it at least be in the small print when you order the DNA test? It's the same as ordering a book for 350.00 and finding it is written in code.
>
> If we are going to bank on 'getting lucky' my money would be on DNA Consultants:
>
> "Our exclusive, best-selling DNA Fingerprint Test examines all your ancestral lines at once, to tell you which countries and ethnic groups your ancestors came from. The test confirms any Native American, African or

183

Asian ancestry."

This careless comparison was the bait for Joy King to take another pot shot at the Jewish Indians. She wrote, "Are you sure this is where you want to put your money?" and pasted the boilerplate from DNA Consultants' "About Us" webpage. Apparently, it was enough to see from Donald Yates' brief company bio mentioning he was "of Choctaw-Cherokee ancestry" for persons of the proper persuasion to take the hint and "run, not walk" in the opposite direction. Now self-fueled, the jubilant cannonade went on for over a hundred more replies and counter-replies in the echo chamber the list had become.

Like many history-making events, the Estes article had one unintended consequence. It would take Indians to recognize the dirty tricks in her research, but the signs were apparent from the beginning. Few realized it, but her sample was trimmed to produce the conclusions she sought. Footnote 4 stated:

> The Melungeon DNA Project, while initially included in this research, was subsequently removed from the report because of the lack of evidence of Native American ancestry and no direct connection to the Lost Colonists. The Lumbee may be connected to the Melungeons, but that remains unproven.

In 2009, Estes went on to publish, "Where Have All the Indians Gone," which brought the predictable weary retort from Indians that they were still here. Estes carried on the tradition of Virginia DeMarce, who, as we saw, favored the BIA's well-honed and time-honored methods for writing people of color out of existence with data and documentation:

> Furthermore, as having Melungeon heritage became desirable and exotic, the range of where these people were reportedly found has expanded to include nearly every state south of New England and east of the Mississippi, and in the words of Dr. Virginia DeMarce, Melungeon history has been erroneously expanded to provide *"an exotic ancestry...that sweeps in virtually every olive, ruddy and brown-tinged ethnicity known or alleged to have appeared anywhere in the pre-Civil War Southeastern United States."*

And so we return full circle to the Office of Recognition. So many impoverished and marginalized brown people actively aware of how their ancestors had been mistreated in the past could spell trouble for government!

Estes then joined Jack Goins, Penny Ferguson and Janet Crain in publishing the long-awaited report on their own Melungeon DNA Project in July 2011. The title of the paper was "Melungeons: A Multiethnic Population." The government vogue word "multiethnic" seems here to have the approximate meaning of not-this, not-that. Y'all can check as many boxes as you like. It won't do you any good. The paper's summary was given as follows:

> Many sources exist where the Melungeons identify themselves variously as Indians and Portuguese. Only one family, the Goins, are (sic) identified orally as having negro (sic) heritage. Given the physically dark

appearance of the Melungeons, they have unquestionable heritage other than European.

Which seemed to be an unsurprising conclusion, until one realized that the authors limited their sights to Ridgers who called themselves Portuguese, and Goins who already identified themselves as having Sub-Saharan African.

Elsewhere in the article, one reads: "The Collins and Gibson founding lines, meaning Vardy Collins and Shephard 'Buck' Gibson were said to be Cherokee and stole the names of white men in Virginia. Their DNA indicates that if they were Native, it was not via their paternal line."

Comma splice. How do you steal a white man's name? I certainly hope no Melungeons are going to steal mine.

Another revelation was: "A link has been found through the Goins family to the Lumbee. The 'Smiling' Goins family was not thought to be an original Lumbee family, but subsequent research has shown that even though the group in 1915 was thought to be an 'outside' group, the ancestors of this group were found in 1770 with other founding Lumbee families." Here was another distinction without a difference.

And finally, the real point of the article:

No evidence, (sic) historical, oral, genealogical or genetic has been found to support a Turkish, Middle Eastern, Jewish or Gypsy heritage.

Roberta Estes' killing off of the Lost Colony "Indians" by the tried-and-true methods of the BIA won her "the Prestigious Paul Jehu Barringer, Jr.

and Sr. Award of Excellence in grateful recognition of her Dedication and Devotion to Preserving and Perpetuating North Carolina's Rich History." Expecting similar accolades for laying to rest the Melungeon "mystery," Goins and his team did achieve national press coverage the minute their work hit print, or rather the WorldWideWeb. But the reaction was not what they had bargained for. What ensued was like a box of flying squirrels being dumped in the living room of a trailer during a tornado or an episode of the "Hatfields and McCoys."

In the aftermath many were glad they did not buy tickets on the Goins trainwreck. But one of the unforeseen effects played out in the American Indian community. "Jack Goins Declares War on Indian Heritage" was the headline, and "Genocide" the watchword, in an infuriated outcry from Scott Collins. Like most observers, Collins thought that the article "postulates that the 'Melungeons' are African Americans" (May 26, 2012):

> This is a total bunk job and shear genocidal activity against the Saponi, Lumbee, Occaneechi, Tutelo, Cherokee, Tuscarora, Haliwa and Powhatan and other Indian peoples of Appalachia. This same tactic was used back in the days of Walter A. Plecker, first registrar of vital statistics of Virginia. Plecker was bent on a campaign to cover Indian ancestry by calling anyone that claimed Indian ancestry to be African American (he used the term Negro at that time). Plecker was a White Supremacist and a member of the Anglo Saxon Club. He wrote and helped push

for the Racial Integrity Act in Virginia.

Lest readers think the word "genocide" was being used recklessly, Collins, a member of a non-federally-recognized American Indian tribe, went on to cite the articles of the Convention on the Prevention and Punishment of the Crime of Genocide. Within the agreed-upon definition of genocide was: causing mental harm to members of the group, deliberately inflicting on the group conditions of life calculated to bring about its physical destruction in whole or in part and imposing measures intended to prevent births within the group.

Virginia DeMarce retired in 2004 after a forty-year career in the Bureau of Indian Affairs' Office of Recognition. She had done her work well, just like Walter Plecker, Charles B. Davenport, William Harlen Gilbert, Jr., Edward T. Price, Calvin L. Beale, Thomas J. Harte and a host of others in the archives of American official racism. The Melungeon Movement was effectively dead.

ANCESTORS AND ENEMIES

*Peter had a wooden leg and
Malinda was a midwife*

11 WHERE DID ALL THE MONEY GO

Abridged from the article, "Sand Mountain Melungeon Families: A DNA Perspective," by Donald Panther-Yates, published online at Melungeons.com in May 2005.

Sand Mountain is a flat-topped extension of the Cumberland Plateau stretching for a hundred miles along the Tennessee River through the states of Tennessee, Georgia and Alabama. Its twin, Lookout Mountain, lies across the valley. Interstate 59 runs alongside from Chattanooga, Tennessee to Fort Payne and Boaz, Alabama, near Blountsville. In ancient times, a mixture of Cherokee, Yuchi, Koasati, Creek and other Indian tribes inhabited the hilly area. The Spanish explorer Hernando De Soto visited its towns in 1539/1540. In the census of 1950, Jackson County was the first white county formed in Alabama from the Cherokee Cession of 1816. In the census of 1950, it had 70 persons identified as Melungeon. This article surveys the genealogies and ancestry of some of these families. Surnames included are Adkins, Beam(er), Black,

Blevins, Brown, Bunch, Bundren, Burke, Burns, Cooper, Davis, Fields, Gist, Gunter, Keys, Lackey, Lowrey, Redwine, Riley, Shankles and Sizemore.

My own interest in the Melungeons of Sand Mountain began in 1997, when in the course of pursuing some genealogy work on my mother's Coopers, I encountered a very strange court record on USGenWeb. It named one of our ancestors, Isaac Cooper, rumored to have been a mixed blood Choctaw-Cherokee who married a daughter of Cherokee principal chief Black Fox (Enola, Inali, died 1811). The record presented Isaac Cooper giving a deposition in the home of James Cooper in newly-formed Jackson County, Alabama. It concerned the Great Salt Works of the Big South Fork of the Cumberland River in Wayne County, Kentucky. What in the world was going on?

After nearly ten years of grappling with this and like issues, I have only one remaining question. *Where did all the money go?* How did our ancestors come to be dispossessed of such a splendid legacy, of their lands, their possessions, their rights? The following notes detail some of the land sales, mineral prospecting, manufacturing, trade activities, lobbying and legal moves of these Melungeon families in an ever-shifting and increasingly complex social environment.

The **Adkins** (also spelled Atkin, Atkinson, Aiken, etc.) were multiply intwined with my pioneer Cooper, Blevins and Burke families from Wayne County, Kentucky. They came from Pittsylvania County, Virginia, an important staging area for the movement of Melungeon families onto the northern and eastern boundaries of the

Cherokee.

Before Virginia, these Adkins are traced to a James Atkinson, a Quaker who came to Philadelphia in the 1600s, probably from a Welsh port. His great-grandson William Adkins left a will dated Jan. 22, 1784, probated March 15, 1784 (D&W Bk. Vol. 11 p.136), and was buried near Cooper's Old Store, Pittsylvania Co., Va. William's son Owen was born about 1750 in Lunenberg County, Virginia (the parent county of Pittsylvania) and died in Watauga, Hawkins County, Tennessee about 1790. He married Agnes Good/Goad, from the same family that provided the spouse of Valentine Sevier (1701/02-1803). They were the parents of John Sevier, the first governor of Tennessee. One of Sevier's his sons, Valentine, married Sarah Cooper. The Seviers go back to Don Juan de Xavier, a Jew who took refuge in Narvarre during the Spanish Inquisition.

In 1836, Benjamin Adkins built a log mill on the Little South Fork of the Cumberland near Parmleysville, Kentucky, made of huge squared logs. This mill, with rifle slits on two levels, is still standing. He left a will in 1839 showing $10,000 in debts owed him and an estate of great value. Numerous family members moved first to Sequatchee (Marion County, Tennessee) and subsequently to Sand Mountain, homesteading a hidden cove at the foot of Fox Mountain called Anawaika, or Deerhead Some went west to Arkansas. William E. Adkins (about 1828-1862) married Susan E. (Sukie) Cooper (about 1831-1901), the daughter of Isaac and Mahala Jane Cooper, April 20, 1847, in Henry County, Tennessee.

Says Steve Akins, "When I was little my Great Grandma Adkins (Virgie Stanley) use to tell me stories about my Great Grandfather's (Arthur 'Aud' Adkins) Grandmother. She said her name was Sukie and she was a Cherokee Indian. I later found out that 'Sukie' was a nickname for Susan. She also mentioned the name Mahala Blevins.

Black is a Scottish name associated with clans Lamont, Macgregor and Maclean. About 1790, Mary Ann Black married William Davis, a Revolutionary War soldier born in Virginia in 1753 who died and was buried in Maynard's Cove on Sand Mountain in 1848. She was a daughter of Black Fox, a lieutenant in Dragging Canoe's Chickamauga army fighting the Tennesseans who later became principal chief or "Cherokee King."

On Chief Black Fox's tomb the following description was written in *An Account of Some Creek, Cherokee and Earlier Inhabitants of Blount County*:

Most of the first settlers of Blount as well as those of the adjoining counties, believed that lead mines existed in Blount and Jefferson counties, and that the Indians knew their location and obtained lead from them. Perhaps, this general belief originated from the following circumstance, which occurred in 1810:

An old Cherokee Chief, named Black Fox, died in the north of our county, and was buried in an old mound; and in digging his grave, the Indians found some pieces of lead ore. This trivial discovery was magnified and circulated in Madison Count, and many intelligent persons in the county believed a lead mine really existed, at, or near the grave of the old Chief. This opinion became so strong, that Alexander Gilbreath, who then resided in Huntsville, was induced to visit the grave of Black Fox. His search there, proving unsuccessful.... Mr. George Fields, at that time fifty or sixty years old, informed him that the Indians knew of no lead mines nearer than those of Missouri and Illinois, and gave it as his opinion, that the lead found in the grave of Black Fox, had been brought from one of those States. John Gunter, (another old inhabitant of the valley, who had been brought up among the Chickasaws, and spent all his life with the Indians,) gave the same opinion, as to the pieces of lead which had been found in different parts of the county, viz: that they had been brought by the Indians from the northern mines. These two persons informed Mr. Gilbreath, that as far back as Indian memory extended, it was the custom of the Creeks to cross the Tennessee river near Deposit, (Baird's Bluff) and make long hunting expeditions, annually to the north, bringing with them, on their return, lead ore. - That the settling of Tennessee by the whites was a great obstacle in their way to the mines - particularly to those of Rock river. - That the Indians had then, in order to reach the mines, to bear lower down the Tennessee river, and that as the whites of Tennessee continued to extend their settlements westward, the difficulties in the way of the Creeks to the mines, were continually increasing. To this account, it may be added, that a company of Creeks, on a returning expedition of the above kind, murdered two or three white families, which led to the Indian war of 1812, at the close of which, they were finally barred from the mines by treaty.

Although it cannot be doubted, that the Indians brought lead ore into Blount from distant mines, yet this fact does not account for the pieces which have been found in the mounds....The mounds above spoken of, are heaps of earth in the form of pyramids. They are supposed to mark the burial places of the Chiefs. Some of them are very old, having upon their tops, growing trees of very large size. These mounds are to be found in thirteen different places in our county. Two or three of them are generally grouped together, or within a half mile of each other. In Murphree's Valley, there is one group consisting of three mounds, from four to seven in height. In the trough of the Locust Fork, there are five distinct groups. In Blountsville Valley, (and near Blountsville) there is one; and in Brown's Valley one. North-west of the Mulberry Fork, there are four groups. These mounds are invariably in the valleys, on, or near the best bodies of land. This fact proves pretty clearly that the Indian settlements were in the valleys. Some knowledge of agriculture, may have led them to settle there, or it may have been the greater abundance of game and water found in such places. About these mounds, great quantities of flint spikes are found, which some persons believe were used as arrow-heads, but they seem unfit for such a purpose. The efficiency of the arrow, depends in a great degree upon its velocity; and arrows of sufficient strength to give great velocity to these spikes, would be so heavy, that all the power of the archer would fail to give them the force requisite to enter the vitals of a large animal.

If we consider them as knives, there would be many uses for them: - such as skinning animals, severing the carcass, scaling fish, and cutting or sawing vegetable substances. Some of these spikes are six inches long, and weigh nearly a pound.

In 1818, Col. Brown went to Washington City for the avowed purpose of selling to the whites, or ceding by treaty, all that portion of country. He advised the Indians to hold themselves in readiness to leave the country on his return. They accordingly assembled at Gunter's Landing, for the purpose of emigrating; but the death of Col. Brown shortly afterwards, (who died at Rogersville, in Hawkins County, Tennessee,) prevented, for many years, the ratification of the treaty, and consequently the removal of the Indians. As soon, however, as it was known that the Indians had collected together with a view to emigrating, the restless whites thronged into the country which they had abandoned, and obtained such hold, that they could never be entirely driven out. Brown's Valley at this time, showed a motley population of Cherokees, Creeks, and whites. The United States troops cut down the growing crops of the whites, and burned their houses; but with all this severity, they were unable to clear the valley of their presence. This portion of territory gave great trouble to the citizens of old Blount, as it prevented the ordinary execution of the laws in many instances . . . . It continued to annoy the people of our county until the year 1832, when the Legislature extended the laws of the State over it.

The **Blevinses** are an old British Jewish family who emigrated in the 1600s to Rhode Island and were later prominent in the vanguard of the settlement of Tennessee and Kentucky. William Blevins, a Long Hunter in Pittsylvania County, married Agnes Walling/Walden, the sister of Elisha Walling (for whom Walden's Ridge is named), and Blevinses were among the signers of the Watauga Purchase on March 19, 1775. Jonathan Blevins (about 1763 – about 1830), like his twin brother Richard, was a Revolutionary War soldier in the Upper New River Valley. During the shift of the Cherokee population southward in the 1820s and 1830s, the two brothers bought land in Marion Co., Tenn. Elections were held in Jonathan's house on the stage road in District 4, Cave Springs, between Sequatchie River, Walden's Ridge and Cumberland Mountain. Jonathan married to Charlotte Muse, the daughter of Richard Muse, a wealthy land agent who disposed of over 2400 acres of land in Montgomery/Wythe/Grayson Co., Va. before settling in what became Campbell Co., Tenn. Most of Jonathan and Lottie Muse's children avoided the Trail of Tears, though a cousin also named Richard Blevins (about 1785 – after 1850) seems to have embraced removal, discarding his white wife for two Jones sisters and moving west to Cape Girardieu, Mo., finally ending up in Texas. Two sisters Lucretia (Creecy) and Mahala Jane (Linny) married two brothers, James and Isaac Cooper, but the two couples were divided in the commotions of the 1830s and 40s, with Lucretia Cooper and her family migrating to Marion Co., Ark., and Jane Cooper and her family managing to remain in the East, in Deerhead Cove. The children of Jonathan's twin brother, Richard (about 1763-

after 1839), who was married to Hannah Osbourne, changed their name to Blevans and pursued a different survival strategy, some moving west to Missouri after spending a few years in Marion Co., Tenn. and Jackson Co., Ala. Throughout all their moves, the Blevins were careful to support other members of their circle. For example, Richard Blevins served as character witness for Jacob Troxell in Marion Co., Tenn. in 1832, before Jacob too moved on to DeKalb Co., Ala., and William Blevins gave an affidavit in 1850 for his widowed sister Jane Cooper in Dade Co., Ga. Jonathan (Jont) Blevins (1779-1863) married Catherine (Katie) Troxell, the daughter of George Jacob Troxell and his Cherokee wife Cornblossom (his brother Tarleton married her sister Mary Polly Troxell), and he was the commander of road work near the Little South Fork River in Wayne Co., Ky.

During the Civil War, many of the Blevins men, being railroaders and Union sympathizers like their Cooper cousins, joined the U.S. cavalry of Tennessee. Afterward, they and their Cooper relatives were forced to leave Deerhead Cove and move to New Hope across the state line on the other end of Sand Mountain. The men are described as fairly tall, lean, of dark complexion, with dark hair and either blue, green or yellow eyes—a physical type similar to Moroccan Jews. Many Blevinses are buried either in Cagle Cemetery in Deerhead Cove or New Hope Cemetery on Sand Mountain.

Blevins DNA proved to be E3b, the second most common Hebrew male lineage after J and a gene type found frequently in Moorish and Berber families.

Brown may originally have been Pardo, a common Converso and Marrano name. The Jewish origins of this Cherokee family can be seen in the names they favored for their children (Alexander, Alice, Rebecca, Cassie, David, Eli, Ephraim, Goldie, Hulda, Isom, Julia, Minnie, Nely, Sarah, Silas, Sylvia, Violet and Zachariah), as well as in their marriage partners' surnames (Barton, Burke, Cooper, Craze, Fields, Frazier, Gilbreath, Guess/Gist, Harris, Hearne, Jean/Jane, Lowrey, Proctor, Ross, Ruth, Sizemore, Vann, White and Yates).

A notable member of the Brown clan was Capt. John Brown, born about 1756, residence Creek Path in 1817. He was a packhorseman for the Cherokee traders, and later a Chickasaw trader and partner of Jerome Courtonne. His sister married Oconostota, the Beloved Warrior of Great Tellico. (Brent Cox, *Heart of the Eagle*, 1999.) Chief Brown died Oct. 24, 1861 in Sallishaw, Indian Territory.

Chief John Ross's (1790-1866) wife was a Brown, and trader Alexander Brown married a daughter of Chief Dragging Canoe, Naky Sarah. There are at least seven Chickamauga Chief Browns, most of them associated with Creek Path. The Browns supplied so many soldiers for the Creek War that their contingent was called "Brown's army." After Horse Shoe Bend, they were granted extensive lands in western Alabama. They operated Brown's Ferry across the Tennessee River near Chattanooga as well as the military road that came in later and were also involved in local ironworks.

A large ironworks had been established by Daniel Ross and Company, in Hawkins Co., Tenn., in the heart of the Watauga Country near the present-day community of Rotherwood. John Ross was captured by the Chickamaugans in Francis Mayberry's boat on the Tennessee River in 1785. John McDonald, the British Indian agent, a Scotsman from Inverness, retained him to help start a trading post and he afterward married McDonald's daughter, Mary, whose mother was a halfblood Cherokee, the daughter of the former interpreter. His son John Ross was McDonald's heir. McDonald and Ross moved from Sequatchie Valley to what became Rossville, Ga. at the foot of Lookout Mountain around 1800 (John P. Brown, *Old Frontiers*).

The first **Bunch** in Melungeon territory (various spellings) was apparently "Trader" John Benge, born about 1735 in Albemarle Co., Va., died about 1800 probably in Georgia. Benge had both a Cherokee and white family, like many of the Coopers, Gists, Beans, Blevinses, Wallings, Wards, Stuarts, Martins and other Jewish merchants of the time. His son by Wurteh (Gurty, a nickname for Margaret), the daughter of Great Eagle, or Willenewah, of Tasagi Town, was the outlaw Chickamauga chief Bob Benge, who probably was responsible for the entry of the word "binge" into the English language. Also known as Captain Bench, and The Bench, he was born in Toqua Town and died on April 9, 1794 in Stone Gap, Va., after being tracked down by a local posse. Wurteh went on to marry Nathaniel Gist, the father of George Guest (Sequoyah, born about 1771 near Fort

Loudon). Benges married into the Brown, Lowrey and Watts families around Chattanooga.

The original form of the name **Bundren** was Bondurant, from a southern French family documented in the area about Narbonne and Avignon as early as the 1400s. Claibourne Peter Bundren (1774-after 1850) was the first to change the spelling to Bundren. All persons in the United States with these names trace back to a single emigrant founder, Jean Pierre Bondurant (1677-1734). Born in a small village in the south of France, Jean Pierre was a Protestant who escaped to Switzerland at age 20 in 1697. He reached Jamestown with about 100 other Huguenot refugees on the "Peter and Anthony" from London in 1700 and settled in Manakin Town, a deserted Indian village on the James River just west of Richmond. He had been trained as an apothecary and practiced medicine in Virginia. He is said to have received 400 acres of land from King George I of England, confirmed in 1725. He and his wife Ann were members of the King William Parish church and had five children. His grave site is located on Birdsong Lane, Spencerwood West, Midlothian, Virginia. It is surrounded by an iron fence and has a marker placed there by the Bondurant Family Association in 1990.

The Bundrens of Sand Mountain raised several large families near Henegar before packing up, lock, stock and barrel, and moving to Kansas in the 1880s. Their original land purchase goes back to Claiborne's purchase in DeKalb Co., Ala., Aug. 19, 1842. Because of their dark complexions, the Bundrens were accused by many on Sand

Mountain of being black.

The **Burkes** were French Sephardic Jews who settled in Virginia, North Carolina, Pennsylvania and Kentucky. John Burke emigrated from Cork, Ireland, to Pennsylvania and his descendants proceeded south to Virginia and North Carolina and west to Kentucky. A James Burges appears in Hawkins around 1797. James Burke, born in County Limerick, Ireland, about 1705, discovered Burke's Garden located in Tazwell Co, Va. in 1753, and is frequently mentioned in local histories of that region. John Burke signed a petition from North of Holston against the so-called Fincastle Petition in 1777. Benjamin Burke (1765-1828) married Elizabeth Troxell (1752-1851), the sister of trader/spy George Jacob Troxell (1758-1843, DeKalb Co., Ala.). They are buried in the Smith-Kidd Cemetery, Great Meadow Community, Rock Creek, McCreary Co., Ky. Surnames of favorite marriage partners are Anderson, Bane, Brown, Blevins, Byatt, Coil (Coyle), Davis, Gregory, Hatfield, Lewellan, Millican, Orr, Smith and Steele.

The annals of the **Cooper** family would fill volumes. Cooper is one of the most common surnames today in the Tri-State Region surrounding Sand Mountain. Though Coopers are generally aware of their "Indian blood" — one living male Cooper with no other Indian bloodlines tested seven percent American Indian, which would place the generation of full-bloods in his ancestry approximately in the early eighteenth century — few know the whole story. It begins in medieval Norman France and becomes linked with the fortunes of Anthony Ashley-Cooper, earl of

Shaftesbury, and Lord High Chancellor of Britain, in the seventeenth century. Before that, the Coopers were country gentry in Herefordshire in Wales, closely allied with the Ross (Rowse, Rose) family and known for their cattle breeding and exemplary public life (Ross, 1932).

Cooper R1b DNA matches Stewart, Ramey and other lines identified as French Levites.

Cooper, Benjamin (born about 1772 in Granville Co., N.C.), first justice of the inferior court, and organizer of a Cherokee school, Gilmer Co., Ga. Married Temperance Simon Lemar of Anjou, France (died about 1809 in the Cherokee Nation East), and later a Cherokee woman called Pretty Girl (U-Wo'-du-a-ge-yu'-tsa). The family received reservation #92 in 1817, reaffirmed in 1819, subsequently canceled. They then emigrated west, arriving in Indian Territory on May 30, 1834, with seven slaves. Died June 26, 1852, Flint District, Cherokee Nation West.

Cooper, Cornelius C. (about 1740-1808), planter and merchant, labeled Free Person of Color in the Fishing Creek District, Granville County, North Carolina.

Cooper, Harmon S(olomon) (1811-1886). Harmon Cooper lived next door to his sister Nancy and brother-in-law Jonathan Burke on the Little South Fork of the Cumberland River, near Nobusiness Creek. Later, this area was cut out of Kentucky and made part of Tennessee. Thus, in later years, he was counted in Fentriss Co., Tenn. Without moving, Harmon Cooper lived in four different counties and two states (*Harmons Cooper & Moses Slagle of Wayne County, Kentucky & Iowa &*

Their Descendants, by Rosalie L Cooper Leavelle, 1983). Harmon is buried in the Cooper Adkins Cemetery in the Mt. Pisgah area. It is a small cemetery in a pine woods. A sign says that it is maintained by descendants of Benjamin Adkins and Harmons Cooper. "Harmon Cooper dressed like a southern gentleman of the 1800's. His dress was usually of dark material and his waistcoat was cut just below the hips with trousers to match with narrow cut legs. His hat was wide brimmed and he wore boots almost to his knees. Harmon married his first wife and they had 15 children. Wayne Co., Ky. was of Union persuasion during the Civil War and was surrounded by Confederate sympathy. Confederate soldiers hanged Harmon, and after they left, his women cut him down. He survived to marry a second time and sire 6 more children." His three wives were Mary Ann Atkins, Mahala Jackson, and Martha Pile. The names of his children were: Meecie, Talitha Leanne, Luida, Catherine, Isaac, Lucinda Jane, John Granville, Benjamin Turner, William H., George Washington, Artemellia (Artie), Milly, James, Cansada, Alvin, Alfred, Victoria, Silas, Rosa, and (youngest) Joseph.

Cooper, Henry Labon (about 1745 – after 1830), wainswright, planter and land developer. During the Revolution, Henry served as a private in the 2nd Corps D'Elite of Green's Virginia Militia from the Watauga Country, under the name Henry Laban. Afterwards, listed as Enrico Labon Cooper (p. 26) his name appears in the "Mobile Names" of San Esteban de Tombecbe (Tombigbe, St. Stephens), and he was one of the North Carolinians on the surrender list of 1781 when the Spanish established control of the hinterlands of Mobile (Enrico Cooper), along with a William (Guilielmo) Cooper: Archivo General de Indias in Seville, previously Havana Cuba (Papelas de Cuba) 2359: 417-18. He took an oath of allegiance and served as corporal together with another Enrico, probably Houston Cooper, his son, and Samuel and William (Guilielmo), brothers, all appearing on a 1787 Spanish census of Second Creek (p. 105, *Anglo Americans in Spanish Archives. Lists of Anglo-American Settlers in the Spanish Colonies of America. A Finding Aid*, by Lawrence H. Feldman, Baltimore: Genealogical Publishing Co., 1991). In 1789, Henry, Samuel & William Cooper were tobacco growers in Second and Sandy Creek, now TN/AL/MS tri-state area (List of Tobacco Growers, Spanish Natchez District, 1790). In one season alone, they grew 21,200 pounds. This became the Tri-state Mussel Shoals area between Corinth, Miss., Florence, Ala. and Waynesboro, Tenn.

Cooper, Huston (about 1767-1833), plantation owner on the Harpeth River in Davidson Co., Tenn. Married to "a quarteroon Indian woman" (Nancy Cooper v. The Choctaw Nation, 1902). He died shortly before the Trail of Tears.

Cooper, Isaac (about 1775 – about 1845). A son of Henry Cooper, Isaac is first attested in the List of Taxes and Taxable property in the bounds of Capt. (William) Bean's Company, returned by William Stone, Esquire, 1799. This was in Cherokee country along the Holston River and Clinch Mountain in Tennessee, later Grainger County, also known as the Watauga Settlement, or State of Franklin. William Bean Sr.'s was the first white cabin in those parts. 1800 May 20: Grainger Deed from Elizabeth Bean and Robert Blair for one hundred acres proven in open court. Let it be registered for Isaac Cooper. (WPA) Grainger County Court Minutes 1796-1801, p. 170. The original indenture is dated Oct. 11, 1799 and was registered July 9, 1800 (Grainger Register of Deeds, Vol. A-B: Sept. 1796-1811, Vol. A, p. 273). It conveyed 100 of an original parcel of 200 acres adjoining his land on German Creek to Isaac Cooper. This was near the second Bean's Station on the saddle of land leading over the ridge of Clinch Mountain called Copper Ridge (prob. after William Cooper, Isaac's grandfather). Two years later, Isaac resold the land to Stephen Brundige (Bunch?) at a handsome profit (Vol. A, p. 259). By 1810, Isaac had moved again. He is listed in the Wayne Co., Ky. 1810 census: COOPER, Isaac 21010-21010-00. In 1814, he was granted a certificate that later entitled him to 4x50 acres (200 total) of land in Wayne County, Ky., pursuant to the treaty with the Cherokee Indians at Tellico (Treaty of Oct. 25, 1805). The land was on the Little South Fork in Tellico Bounds, on Lonesome Creek. The survey for his tract was dated June 10, 1815. Beginning about the same time, he gradually bought parcels of land in Sumner Co., near Gallatin. In 1820, as the Cherokee continued to be squeezed south, he left Wayne County, Ky. for Jackson Co., Ala., and in 1830 he is found living on the Sumner Co. land.

Cooper, Isaac (about 1804-1847) was a mixed blood Cherokee-Choctaw and Jewish railroader from Kentucky who died during the Mexican War in Vera Cruz, Mexico. He is buried in or near the

Church of San Francisco, built 1775, once part of a Franciscan convent, then used as a hospital by the American army during the 1847-1848 occupation of Vera Cruz. It is located in the port area, near the Plaza de la Reforma. He married Mahala Jane Blevins of the Long Hunter Blevins family, and she received a widow's pension.

Isaac Cooper bought 50 acres of land on Beaver Creek in Wayne Co. around 1824. The survey was dated Jan. 29, 1824. He then bought land in Marion Co., Tennessee, in the 1830s. He had moved there about 1825. He is counted in the 1830 census on page 58. There were seven in his household: 3 males under 5, 1 male 5-10 years old (Jackson Cooper?), 1 female under 5 and his wife 20-30 years old (Jenny Blevins?). He is mentioned as a landholder on Sequatchie Creek, Marion Co. Deed Book, p. 319. In 1831, he sold land in district four to Mary Porter and her family for $100. About 1838, he settled in Deerhead Cove, Dade County, Ga., on the Alabama line (DeKalb Co.)

Isaac Cooper also evidently served in the Cherokee Wars during the latter part of the 1830s. There is a private by that name in Dossett's Company of 3rd Battalion of the Tennessee Infantry, also in Powell's Co. of Lindsay's Regiment of 1st Tennessee Mounted Volunteers. Many "friendly" Indians and halfbreeds joined the army and helped remove the Cherokees, often as scouts. Isaac would probably have been considered a Choctaw quarter-breed and not a Cherokee.

In 1833, while her husband Zack was away at war, Mrs. Cooper, said to be extremely beautiful, was raped while at her job by the railroad foreman, a McDaniel. Mariah Ann Cooper was born nine months later and raised as the Coopers' own daughter. In the Civil War, Mariah Ann was sent for safety to Ashe Co., N.C. She never married. She died in 1927 and is buried in Bondtown Cemetery, Coeburn, Va.

Isaac Cooper bought land on cash sales from the Lebanon land office in Dekalb Co., Ala., Sec. 27, Tsp. 3S, Range 10E (next to James Blevins, apparently right across the state line from Deerhead Cove, Dade Co., Ga.) on two occasions: June 1, 1845 and April 10, 1847 (80 and 40 acres). In August of 1847, he enlisted in the army.

According to Billie Groening, Isaac Cooper joined the army August 5, 1847, in Dade Co., and was a private in Calhoun's Battalion (D Company, Calhoun's Mounted Battalion, Georgia Infantry). His brother William was in the same outfit as a scout.

According to Isaac's grandson Peter Cooper, "My grandmother Jane Cooper always said that the Indian Chief Fox always claimed to be akin to Grandfather Isaac Cooper" (Peter Cooper ECA docket). Peter Cooper also said, "They, Father and Grandfather, were recognized as white folks when they lived. They lived with white people. Never heard of them living with the Indian tribe except that they were in this state when the Indians left. They did not leave when the Indians left. I don't know why the Indians left." (Peter Cooper Testimony in care of George A. Cooper #41086 supplementing Application #19589, July 1, 1908). Isaac was called Zack by the family, and his wife, Linny. Peter Cooper's ECA was rejected, appealed, and rejected again.

Cooper, Jackson (1824-about 1879). According to Lily Wigley, nee Cooper, in 1907, "Grandfather Jack Cooper was enrolled, so I am informed. He, it is said, was of Cherokee blood." John Floyd Sizemore, Mary Ann Cooper's brother, mentions Jackson Cooper in a letter written to William C. Sizemore from Camp Springs, Tennessee, May 7, 1863: "Tell Stoner and Jackson Cooper to write to me and not be so dull no more." Jackson Cooper cannot be found in the 1860 census, though his large family does appear in the Alabama 1866 census, living in Fractional Township 4, Range 9 E in Jackson County (Sand Mountain). They were also counted in the same township in DeKalb County as J. Cooper. Their neighbors were Henegars, Thompson, Sizemores and Schraders. Their land straddled the county line. Lily Wigley's ECA 42035, along with those of her siblings and cousins, was denied. Jackson Cooper lived with his wife Mary Ann Sizemore and others, including Blevinses and Holloways in Shellmound, Tenn. He is listed as blind on the 1870 census.

Cooper, James (about 1795-1848) Isaac and Nancy Cooper's first-born, considered to be Cherokee-Choctaw of the Paint Clan, but moving primarily in the white world, deposed his brother Isaac Cooper on October 8, 1821 at his home in Jackson Co., Alabama. At that time, the Tennessee River formed the boundary with Cherokee Lands, which included Sand Mountain. His home and improvements "on Wills Creek across the ridge from Copelands Mill" adjoining Eli Cooper was assessed in the fall of 1833 or spring of 1834 in accordance with the 1828 treaty with the Cherokee Nation. It consisted of 1 house (18 x 16) made of hewn logs with a board roof and plank floor "neated sealed with boards nailed on inside...1 door well cased and faced with plank, small window faced, joists and board loft...chimney well walled with Stone and Stone hearth." Outbuildings included a log kitchen, smokehouse, corn crib, two other cribs, hog lot, yard lot and garden lot "well fenced" (Valuations under the Treaty of 1828, Special Collections, Library, University of Tennessee Knoxville, No. 44, pp. 355-56). In the meantime, James Cooper received 50 acres on the Little South Fork of the Cumberland River, Wayne Co., Ky., March 12, 1823, augmented by 50 more acres, Feb. 2, 1825. His daughter Jenny was born in Kentucky in 1824; she later married John Andrew Craze of a family that lived near the Keyses on Craze Bend in the Fabius area of Sand Mountain. In 1832, he was in Marion Co., Tenn. and by 1833, Rutherford Co., where Edith, his daughter, was born, after a brief stay in Meigs Co. Previously, he had been authorized "to hawk and peddle" in Campbell Co. in 1823 (--Acts of Tennessee). Also, he had been appointed in Campbell Co. to the Powells Valley, Jacksborough and Knoxville Turnpike Co. (174.16). His daughter Martha G. Cooper, who married Granville C. Carter, son of Charles Wesley Carter and Hannah Berry, was apparently born in Virginia, in 1836. In the early 1840s, James Cooper was deeded land by Gaines Blevins, his brother-in-law, on Sand Mountain, where he and Creecy's youngest child, Julia Cooper, was born about 1842, but this was later sold or forfeited. James Cooper moved to the Limestone area of Marion Co., Arkansas with the Adair family about 1843, their route westward taking them through Kentucky, Virginia, Ohio, Indiana, Illinois, and Missouri, and died there about 1848, leaving a widow and six children.

Cooper, Mary (about 1809-1834), married Thompson Sinard, great-grandson of fullblood Cherokee woman known as Leek and James Sinard of North Carolina, a descendant of the Huguenot religious dissenter Chevalier de Sinard, who came to America via Ireland. The Sinards were lapsed Quakers and among the first settlers of Buncombe Co., N.C. James Thomas Sinard died in Collinsville, DeKalb Co., Ala., about 1850. Harriet L. Sinard married William Henry Atkins. There was a connection with the namesake for Big Wills Valley outside Valley Head, and Little Wills and Little Wills Creek, both the north branch and the south branch, which meander across Little Wills Valley and through the town of Collinsville. William Webber, also called Redheaded Will, was the son of a Cherokee woman, the mother also, by Kittegunsta, of Ostenaco, and a British officer named Webber. He came from Nequassee in North Carolina. His half-sister was Margaret Siniard, who married a Lamb. Some researchers have Margaret as the daughter of Anawaika (Deerhead). His brother may have been Archibald Webber, and he was somehow related to Blackheaded Cooper, Mary Cooper's father, also recorded as a Chickamauga chief. The Webbers intermarried with the Vanns, too. Sarah Webber married John Brown. Chief Will's daughter Betsy Webber married Chief John Looney. Their daughter Eliza Abigail Looney married Daniel Rattling Gourd. Another daughter, Eleanor, married Gen. Elias (Stand) Watie. Yet another daughter, Rachel, married John Nave, the grandson of Daniel Ross and Mary McDonald.

Cooper, Nancy (1803-1880), third daughter of Isaac and Nancy Cooper of Wayne Co., Ky. Married Jonathan Burke, separated in 1850, widowed in 1876. "In the 1880's Peter Burke [Nancy and Jonathan Burke's son] loaded an ox wagon and took his mother Aunt Nancy and went to Oklahoma. They were nine weeks on the road. Aunt Nancy rode through on a little bay mare whose name was Teen. I can't forget how she looked when I last saw her. Her last words to my mother were, and I quote, 'Farewell, we'll meet again.'" (W.H. "Huse" Blevins, 1869-1964). Nancy never made it to Indian Territory, where they had Choctaw relatives. She is believed to have died and be buried in the town of Temple, Bell Co., Texas.

Cooper, Peter Isaac (1843-1914), railroader, disabled Civil War soldier. Discharged April 5, 1862 at Yorktown, Va. because he lost a leg. He lived on the old Sellars Place on Sand Mountain five miles south of Long Island and was a sharecropper in Cherokee Co., Ala. and in Jackson Co., Ala. for Ike Hembree. Married Malinda (Lindy) Elizabeth Sizemore, who lived to be over 90 years old and served as midwife for Sand Mountain families (including the author's mother's).

Cooper, William Labon (1805-1860), second lieutenant, Capt. Fulton's Company D Mounted

Georgia Volunteers, in the Mexican War where he served as scout. Married Sarah Glass, daughter of Thomas Glass and granddaughter of Chief Glass, and the family moved to Wilkes Co., N.C. After his brother Isaac's death, he took care of widow Mahala Jane Cooper in Anawaika. On one of his trips to visit her, he was shot and killed in July 1860 in Dade Co., Ga. (Mortality Schedule).

Cooper, William (1807-1859), son of Thomas Cooper, R.S., born October 19, 1762, in Chester Co., Penn., and Mariah Burton of Fentress Co., Tenn. Campbell Co., p. 218, 1100010000000 000001010000. The female b. 1770-1780 in William's household in Campbell Co., Tenn. 1830 is probably his mother, Thomas' widow, half Cherokee. Joined other Coopers in Anawaika, Ala./Ga. and is listed on the DeKalb Co., Ala. 1840 census. In 1850, he was acting justice of the peace. He was murdered in 1859 (Mortality Schedule, 1860). Son **James Cooper**, married to Lucinda Hawkins of McMinn Co., Tenn., was elected DeKalb County constable in 1884. He and his family were living in T4 10E of DeKalb County in the 1866 Alabama state census.

Cooper, William (about 1820-1847), first-born of Isaac and Jane (Blevins) Cooper. The military records show that Pvt. William Cooper, Co. K, was killed in action at the battle of Cerro Gordo, Mexico, April 18, 1847. He was in the Second Division under Gen. Twiggs, Colonel Harney's First Brigade Mounted Rifles. His widow, Susan Burke, then married his brother James back in Deerhead Cove, Ala., another example of Levirate law.

William **Davis** was born about 1753 in

Hanover Co., Va. He fought in the Revolution and filed for pension, cert. #31986, issued by the Alabama agency, Sept. 18, 1842, under the act of June 7, 1832. In 1787, he signed the State of Franklin petition as William Daves, and he appears on the 1790 tax list in Hawkins Co., Tenn. Around that time, he married Mary Ann Black, a daughter of Black Fox, who had briefly been married to a trader by the name of Pogue. Gen. John Sevier, governor of Tennessee, 1796-1801, mentions "Davis" as a prominent Chickamauga chief.

On William Davis' tombstone in Proctor Cemetery, Maynards Cove, Jackson Co., Ala. is: Alabama Pvt Lindsy's Va Regt. Rev. War. According to secondhand information, "In his pension application William Davis stated that he was acquainted with Col. James Lewis in Albemarle County, Va., who resided later in Franklin Co, Tenn. A letter from Col. Lewis stated that he and William Davis were boys in the same neighborhood. The history of Albemarle County, Va. gives the location of Col. James Lewis' residence as being on the western part of the present University of Virginia. William Davis also stated in his pension application that he lived in Albemarle County, Va. at the time of his enlistment." William Davis lived to be 95.

His son **William Alexander Davis** also became a chief, marrying the daughter of Chief Arthur Burns about 1830. William Alexander Davis was born about 1790, probably in Tennessee. He married Susan Morgan, a white woman, about 1810. A daughter by his first wife is said to have disavowed her father because he later married an

Indian woman (Mary Burns). In 1817, he signed the treaty of July 8 as Young Davis, between Charles Hicks and Saunooka. He signed the treaty of New Echota as William A. Davis (1835). After the death of Chief Arthur Burns, his father-in-law, William Alexander Davis became chief of the Cherokee in Jackson County, inheriting the North Sauty reservation near Blowing Cave, comprising 640 acres, an entire section of land. On October 19, 1837, he sold this to Jesse French for $1.00 an acre (Jackson Co., Deed Book A, p. 172). At this time, he was a medical doctor, schoolteacher and planter, and his property on Sand Mountain was evaluated at $3,887.00, as printed in the Acts of Congress, p. 277. The loss was substantial. In 1838, the family went over the Trail of Tears to Oklahoma. They are listed on the Drennan Roll of 1851. Son John Lowrey Davis married Nancy Turkey. Son William Henry Davis married Eliza Lowrey (Emmet Starr, Oolootsa 1-1-1-7-1-5, p. 368). Daughter Mary Elizabeth Davis married Robert Harrison Akin. Two other daughters married Mayes brothers.

Davis, Davie, Dow, Davidson and their various forms constitute one of the most common Levite names in Scotland and Wales. The DNA is usually R1b.

The progenitor of the large **Fields** family on Sand Mountain came from England. In 1837, when most of the Cherokees around Creek Path were forced into a stockade in Fort Payne, Richard Fields's farm was evaluated at $2611.00, as published in the acts of Congress, p. 13 (277). He had married Susannah Emory, a mixed blood descendant of Ludovic Grant, one of the first

Scottish traders in Cherokee country (1725). Grant's "morganatic" marriage to Elizabeth Tassel of the Long Hair Clan is said to have been the first intermarriage between a British officer and chief's daughter. Susannah's sister, Elizabeth, married 1) Robert Due, 2) John Hellfire Rogers, 3) Tahlonteeski, and 4) Chief John Jolly, the adoptive father of Gen. Samuel Houston.

Gunter: Guntersville and Lake Guntersville are named after this Scottish trading family who intermarried with the Cherokee and resided in Creek Path. Samuel Gunter married Katherine Ghi-go-ne-li of the Paint Clan, and his brother Edward (Ned) Gunter (died 1843, Tahlequah, I.T.) married 1) Elise McCoy, and 2) Letitia Keys. Like the Keyses and Coopers, the family became split between the east and the west during Indian Removal. Augustus Gunter (1815-1894) was agent for the N.C.& St.L. Railroad in Bridgeport. According to the *Cherokee Advocate*, 19 Oct. 1844, George Washington Gunter had erected a cotton gin at his place on the Arkansas River, 15 miles from Ft. Smith, the first in the Cherokee Nation.

The **Keys/Kee** family was evidently Sephardic Jewish in origin. Many were noted as "bright mulattoes," or "other free" in Virginia and North Carolina records of the 18th century. They appear to have been early mixed with Indian. In 1817, when a choice was given to the Cherokee to settle on a reservation in the east for life or emigrate west, Samuel Keys and his three sons Isaac, William and Samuel received reservations on Sand Mountain. During Indian Removal, some Keyses managed to stay in Alabama, others went on the

Trail of Tears. Richard Keys (Chapman Roll 1686) lived for a while in Fabius on Sand Mountain before moving to Indian Territory with his large family. He died February 6, 1892, and was buried in Paw Paw Bottoms, Muldrow, Sequoyah, I.T. He is the Dick Keys named as a character witness on Peter Cooper's ECA. Richard Riley Keys (1813-1884), a brother of Letitia Keys, who was married to Minerva Nave, served as Judge on the Cherokee Nation Supreme Court. Samuel Riley Keys, born 1819, Fabius, married Mary Hannah Easter, a Choctaw.

Richard **Sizemore** came from Spartanburg District, S.C.and moved to Habersham Co., Ga. by 1822 and to Dade County, Ga. about 1845, where he joined a group of other mixed breeds avoiding removal near Rising Fawn. To credit descendants and relatives in Eastern Cherokee claims 1906-1924, which comprise two entire volumes of the Guion Miller Commission's Report, the family came from North Carolina and Virginia and were Cherokee. The name comes from Hungarian Czismar, English Seasmar/Sismor, meaning "bootmaker" in Turkish. They were Portuguese Jews who came from London to Barbados and Jamestown, where they blended with the Saponi, Powhatan, Mattaponi, Cherokee and Creek on the frontier.

Richard Sizemore is buried in Pea Ridge Cemetery, DeKalb Co., Ala. on top of the mountain. This cemetery also contains the graves of Coopers and Bundrens. His widow Elizabeth moved to Fraction Township in the area known as Shraders Mill, where her neighbors were the Coopers and Shraders (Alabama 1866 State Census). She was the daughter of Francis Forester and a Chickahominy woman and died May 01, 1879.

Very recent efforts spearheaded by Alan Lerwick of Salt Lake City, Utah, have traced the Sizemores back to a Michael Sismor, a London merchant who died in 1685. Lerwick has also mapped two distinct DNA lines in Virginia and North Carolina, one continuing the original R1b gene type and the other an American Indian Q haplotype. He believes—and I agree with him—that Indian descent entered the Sizemore family with Henry Sizemore, born about 1698. The descendants of Henry's older brother Ephraim are R1b.

So what do we learn about Sand Mountain Melungeons? Our rather random survey contains: 24 untimely deaths, 6 murders, 2 hangings, 1 rape, 4 divorces, 4 instances of congenital deafness or blindness, an average migration rate of 4.2 moves per lifetime during the period of Indian removal, 6 cases of lost treasure, and uncounted examples—whether aimed at individuals or groups—of theft, assault, imprisonment, legal sanctions, denial of rights, law suits, discrimination and disinheritance. Families were split down the middle, with many members simply vanishing. A large number of sons and daughters chose never to marry. The average lifespan for a female in my mother's direct line, which goes back to a Cherokee woman born about 1790, is 32. Elders were often unwilling to even speak of their losses. In the face of systematic and relentless prejudice, they maintained what they could of their heritage, culture and religious practices, often in a secretive fashion.

Mingo in "Daniel Boone"

12 DYING CAMPFIRES

Abridged from "Dying Campfires: Jews, Indians, and Descendant Organizations," The International Journal of Diverse Identities *12 (2012) 25-36.*

Indigenous people of North America are found throughout British and American fiction, from Caliban in Shakespeare's *The Tempest* and Chief Broom in Ken Kesey's *One Flew Over the Cuckoo's Nest* to Iroquois cult researcher Eva Blindhawk Broussard in Abigail Padgett's mystery novel *Strawgirl.* Two works, however, invite our special attention because of their juxtaposition of Indians and Jews. These are American author Bernard Malamud's posthumous, unfinished novel *The People* and George Tabori's German-language novella and play *Weisman und Rotgesicht* ("Weisman and Copperface: A Jewish Western"). Both appeared in 1989, and both deal, albeit very differently, with the theme of Jews and Indians.

The first is a historical tall-tale modeled on Chief
Joseph and the Nez Percé Indians. The second is a
thoroughly contemporary story set in New Mexico.
Both writers come from a Central European Jewish
background.

Falling at the end of a long and distinguished
career, *The People* does not seem to fit with
anything Malamud ever attempted before. Its
setting is historical, not contemporary, unlike most
of his previous work. The framework takes us back
over a hundred years to the 1870s. Its material is
equally uncharacteristic, for here is a rip-snorting
action tale about a Jewish peddler named Yozip
kidnapped by Indians in the Wild West.
Malamud's usual work focuses on urban Jews. In
place of the somber reality of tenement houses,
sweatshops and grocery stores, we have a weird
folktale, a romantic fable with hardly a naturalistic
detail in it. The only thing *The People* does have in
common with novels like *The Assistant* and *Dubin's
Lives* is its rich humor and vein of *mentschlekhayt*, a
Yiddish word that means "humanity."

The plot of *The People* unfolds around the year
1870. Yozip Bloom, a bumbling peddler and
sometime "copitner" (carpenter) with a thick
accent, is wandering through the West with a
decrepit wagon and horse named Ishmael. One
day, "in a burst of imagination," he bids adieu to
wagon and horse, plucks a gold nugget from a
streambed and sets off to discover what is wrong
with his life. In a town fifty miles east of Pocatello
in Washington State two bad guys shoot his hat off
and attempt to make him do a Jew's dance, but
Yozip fells them both with a quick left hook. As a

reward he is made the town's new unwilling sheriff.

Yozip is then kidnapped by Indians, who carry him off gagged and blindfolded to a secluded valley. Their old chief wants to recruit Yozip as the People's advocate to uphold their cause with the lying, thieving, murdering Americans. After passing a series of initiation tests, Yozip becomes a dubious brave. When the old chief dies, Yozip is named his successor. Unsuccessful in talking sense to the Americans, he leads the People on a mad lunge through Montana, just ahead of the U.S. cavalry. This part of the novel is patterned on the abortive escape to Canada by Chief Joseph of the Nez Percé, celebrated for his speech, "From where the sun sits today I will fight no more." Meanwhile, Jozip, as he is now called, has a romantic entanglement with the old chief's daughter, One Blossom, and a series of violent confrontations with the other braves, foremost among them Indian Head. The Indians' bid for freedom ends with a devastating massacre. Jozip surrenders on behalf of the tribe, the Indians are shipped off in cattle cars to a reservation in Kansas, and he returns to Chicago. Here he at first joins a circus as a White Indian but later "enrolls in night school to study law in order to help the Indians fight persecution and injustice."

There are many comic episodes in *The People,* but perhaps the funniest is the initial meeting between Sheriff Yozip and the old Chief Joseph. Yozip is released from his fetters to find himself in a "tall teepee that rose like a mast above the earth."

After relieving his bladder, he turns to the "weather-faced" chief.

> The old Indian cast off his ceremonial bonnet with a suppressed yawn... The chief grunted. He touched a finger to himself, then to Yozip. "We meet equal."
> Yozip agreed in principle.
> "We seek to do what the Great Spirit told us when this earth fell from the ocean sky. The sun and moon were candles. All men come from the Great Spirit, who made us born as men. His name is Quodish. Man spoke his words. They spoke then in one tongue. Quodish is the sun who is sacred.
> "Is it not so?" he asked Yozip.
> "To me this is reasonable," Yozip answered. "And if a man tulks to me reasonable I don't say to him no..."
> "You must speak my words to the white man," said the chief .
> "Me? Yozip?"
> "You, with your name."
> "As the moons change so does the world change. I have told my braves that the old moons are gone, and now is the time for new change, but never of our forests or sky."
> The chief nodded and Yozip nodded. They were sitting cross-legged on the ground.
> "We are an ancient tribe," said the chief. "Some call us the first of this land. Our ancestors said they were the children of

Quodish. We live in his word. We speak his name in our hearts. We touch our heads when we think of him. I say my words to him. Do you understand what I mean?"

"Of cuss," said Yozip, though he did not say what the words might mean.

"We are descended from the first tribe."

"This I understand. From the first comes the second."

"Where do you come from?" asked the chief.

"I come from Russia. I am a socialist."

"What is socialist?"

"We believe in a better world. Not to hurt but to help people."

"These are our words too," said the old chief. "We are the People."

"Amen," said Yozip.

This scene introduces several similarities between Jews, who are the disadvantaged and despised people of Europe, and Indians, their downtrodden equivalents in the New World. It establishes pacifism as a quality Yozip and the old chief both have in common. And it brings the first mention of Quodish, a word that reminds us of *kaddish*, the Hebrew word for blessing. Ironically, the scene also lays bare societal illusions and personal delusions about Jewish and Indian identity.

At one point Yozip asks, "But how can I be an Indian if I was born in Zbrish, in Russia?" The old chief counters that his "true color" is red (a definition of Indian as well as communist). The two are natural brothers and symbolically carry the same name. When Yozip goes to Washington to argue the People's case before the government, the Indian Commissioner questions his ancestry with the sneer, "Do you refer to American Indians or to Hebrews," implying the two have nothing to do with each other. Yozip is anguished. He leaves the Commissioner's presence as "a half-ass Hebrew Indian."

Gradually, Jozip/Yozip accepts his fate and even begins to assert a sort of Indian character, much as Frank in *The Assistant* overcomes his fears and hatred and becomes a Jew, marrying Morris the storekeeper's daughter. Malamud's fiction is full of such unlikely cases of people finding themselves. The human experience as lived by a Jew provides his usual basic subject matter, and being Jewish is often a central metaphor. He once said, "There are more Jews around than one sees or knows of. And because I think this is so I have defined a Jew as a person who wants to be one." All Jews, then, are Jews by choice. In *The People*, however, Malamud gives this theme a twist. The main character becomes an Indian because he wants to be one. He is an Indian by choice and cannot do otherwise. The beauty of the Indian way of life, represented by his love of One Blossom, dictates the stern morality and quasi-religious affirmation and commitment Yozip finds in the end. It is a transcendent metamorphosis fraught with ambiguity both for him and for others – the Indians, the government and the public, who marvel at the White Indian in Buffalo Bill's Wild West Show.

It is a pity the novel was not finished. The last few scenes were planned to include a blessing pronounced on the fallen maiden One Blossom, in other words a sort of mourner's kaddish for the vanished People. This was to be followed by a "Hasidic' dance of the recovered self," thus effectively fusing Jewishness and Indianness. The end of the novel was to be a "rejoicing of life when the self seems annealed." Jew and Indian were to be perfectly and naturally joined. What began as a jokey fable will end as a mystical experience. "In remembering [our ancestors], the artist awakens in himself compassion for their memory as well as for all suffering humanity; and in doing so affirms the value of the individual human life," wrote Malamud. All illusion or delusion was to be overcome.

Though Malamud's choice of American Indians as a foil for the Jewish ethos may strike us as singular to the point of being odd, he did not write in a total vacuum. He followed a very well-worn tradition. The three giants of twentieth-century American Hebrew poetry all cultivate this theme. The first to do so was Benjamin Nahum Silkiner. His Indian epic titled *Mul ohel Timmura* (Before the Tent of Timmura) appeared in 1910. After him came Israel Efros (1891-1971), who used Native American motifs in a more naturalistic way in a historical poem about the Jewish Pocahontas (*Silent Wigwams*, 1933). The third, Ephraim E. Lisitzky (1885-1962), wrote an ambitious epic of more than 300 pages cast somewhat dubiously in the thumping meter of Longfellow's *Hiawatha* (*Dying Campfires*, 1937). Lisitzky later turned his hand to a collection of poems about the black experience, *In the Tents of Kush* (1953).

In addressing such themes, these émigré intellectuals show they recoiled from the crass materialism of the United States and found congenial alter egos in the country's marginalized minorities. They gravitated to Indians because Indians were the most attractive novelties the New World had to offer them in the way of content. Indians represented unconquered material that could give the emerging medium of Hebrew poetry a distinctively American flavor. Moreover, among European Jews, the Lost Tribes theory was not completely dead. Silkiner, Efros and Lisitzky transformed "into a strange yet potent truth the misbegotten notion... that the Indians were Jews," according to the critic Michael Weingrad.

For Silkiner, the figure of the Indian becomes "a dark mirror in which the poet could contemplate the most extreme Jewish hopes and fears," writes Weingrad. The conquest of his fictional Silent Tribe by the brutal Spaniards functions for him as a meditation on the possibility of Jewish annihilation in his own day. The tale of the hero Mugiral is "a chronicle of his own soul." In exactly the same way, Efros uses the image of the Indian as "a product of the author's personal concerns." His story of Tom, a young English painter, who falls in love with the daughter of a Nanticoke Indian chief, Lalari, is "deeply infected... by Jewish history." Sadly, the Indians in all these works by American Hebrew poets meet tragic ends; not a few commit suicide.

Lisitzky pays homage to Indians, too, though his treatment of them is generic and sentimental, according to Weingrad. Thus, in a shallow construct of illusionary thinking, we find them living their lives in innocence and righteousness, hunting their game, catching their fish, fighting their wars and smoking their peace-pipes, singing their songs, dancing their dances, and raising up prayer to "the Great Spirit."

Lisitzky's white men are equally banal figures, arrogant, hypocritical and cruel. Although he draws from authentic folktales – Ojibwe, Seneca, Mohawk, Onondaga, Shawnee, Kwakiutl, Hopi, Menominee, Cree and Algonkin, among others – his Indians are all the same. True to his upbringing in the values of *haskalah* (the humanistic enlightenment period of assimilating European Jewry), Lisitzky gently civilizes them and silently improves them. In a sense, they are turned into good Jews. One of his heroes, Nanpiwati, becomes a champion of peace and brotherhood, but is then victimized in a way that would appeal to the Jewish love of martyrdom. The analogy with Judaism becomes unavoidable in the tale of how the people cooperatively push up the sky to make more room for human existence. Lisitzky explicitly links this to the destiny of the Jewish nation since Sinai. On a different occasion he returns to the same parable to make a point that it is Jews who have the responsibility of raising skies. This is perhaps a reference to the concept of *tikkun olam*, or perfecting the world. Weingrad believes he "merely uses an Indian tale for Jewish purposes," oblivious that this leaves him open to the charge of "cultural imperialism, exploiting selected Indian tales to foist upon them Western values, ethical precepts, morals or messages which are otherwise seldom, if ever, enunciated."

Not only in literature but also in society, American Jews have maintained a high degree of sympathy with Indians. The list of those who have advanced their cause is impressive. It ranges from the founders of the New York-based advocate group Association on American Indian Affairs and Felix Cohen, creator of the authoritative *Handbook of Federal Indian Law*, to Professor Stan Steiner, architect of Native American Educational Services College in Chicago, the country's only institution of higher education chartered, owned, staffed and attended exclusively by American Indians.

If Malamud's hero is a Jew who becomes an Indian, the next protagonist is best understood as an Indian who becomes a Jew — perhaps in a delusional sense. Copperface in George Tabori's *Weisman und Rotgesicht* (1989) is a more deliberate and thought-provoking blend of the two ethnic types. This "Jewish Western," as the subtitle calls it, dramatizes an encounter in modern-day New Mexico between Holocaust survivor/underwear salesman Arnold Weisman and the half-breed Rotgesicht. The German word means literally Redface, but it is translated in the English version of the play as Copperface. Weisman and his "Mongoloid" daughter (we are quoting the language of the play) Ruth are headed for New York City with an urn containing Mrs. Weisman's ashes, which in accordance with her wishes they intend to scatter in a park at the corner of Riverside Drive and 99th Street. Leaving the main highway, they get lost in the desert around Santa Fe, where a

hunter steals their car and leaves them to be
rescued by an Indian who rides up on a mule. This
is Rotgesicht, who tells them he is the descendant
of a Cherokee chief. As is revealed in time,
however, he is actually Geegee Goldberg, the
product of a mixed marriage between a "squaw"
named Juanita and a wandering Jew named
Goldberg. This incongruity is probably inspired by
the real-life story of the Jewish Indian chief
Solomon Bibo, who married the Acoma Pueblo
woman Juana.

In the climax of the piece, an act of the play
titled "High Noon," Weisman and Rotgesicht have
a contest of words and exchange boasts about all
the suffering endured by their respective peoples.
Weisman drops dead of a heart attack, Ruthie
dumps her mother's ashes on her father's head and
rides off with Rotgesicht. We come to realize the
mule represents the hybrid nature of Rotgesicht's
mixed parentage, just as Ruth's being called a
"Mongoloid" pokes fun at the "Mongolian" origin
of Indians.

According to critic Lilian Friedberg, Tabori's
subversive slapstick raises not only the "Jewish
Question" of how Jews should lead their lives, but
also the "Indian Question." Both are handled
provocatively, without any definite resolution. The
action of the play skids and swerves along in "a
complex network of persecutory and racist
mechanisms, both internal and external, that lead
to the situation in which Indian identity [is
challenged] by the dominant culture in much the
same way as Jewish identity in the Diaspora,"
writes Friedberg. Tabori adopts a Native American

perspective to explore the question of identity much as Malamud operates from an explicitly Jewish point of view.

One character in Tabori's *Cannibals* casually observes, "You do not become a Jew. You are reminded of being one." The same could be said of Tabori, who never set foot in a synagogue in his life and was seven-years-old before his family even told him of his Jewish heritage. Like many Jews of the disintegrating Austro-Hungarian Empire the Taboris were thoroughly secularized. They converted to Catholicism, though they were non-believers and non-practitioners in that faith as well—Crypto-Jews in reverse. Indeed, given the realities of Holocaust-era Hungary, one might question whether it was delusional of the family *not* to identify as Jewish.

Despite his dissembled origins, though, most of Tabori's work deals on some level with Jewishness and anti-Semitism. These themes are pursued against a philosophical backdrop that often raises the question: Which is better, to be a victim or a perpetrator? Such a question underlies Weisman and Rotgesicht's duel of wits, with each striving to prove he has a monopoly on suffering. It is little more than a "pissing contest" until Rotgesicht suddenly confesses his bastard Jewish parentage. The tension in the play comes from our uncertainty about his identity, of course. As Friedberg puts it, "It is not quite clear whether Rotgesicht is a self-hating Jewish actor in Redface or a self-deprecating Indian actor in Whiteface." Finally, Rotgesicht is unmasked as a half-breed Jew, a "redface minstrel." He wins the contest.

As the counterfoil to Weisman, Rotgesicht is neither red, nor white nor Jew. He is a "son of a bitch," which is actually the title of a previous version. And so he rides off into the sunset with his retarded bride on the Road to Nowhere, escaping the world of ethnic illusion and delusional identity altogether. It is a scathing, but somehow satisfying, conclusion in what may as well have been a Western concocted by Mel Brooks and Franz Kafka.

The figure of Rotgesicht with his complicated identity raises an interesting point. Jewish Indians *as* Jewish Indians are subject not just to a double but to a quadruple form of misunderstanding. We see the double form in the way in which Yozip/Jozip, his very name a dichotomy, is challenged by the commissioner in Washington and taunted by the two outlaw brothers. Neither anti-Semitism nor the "metaphysics of Indian hating" (Melville's phrase) needs to be explained. They are familiar enough. What compounds the situation are the other two varieties of racism: Jew against Jew and Indian against Indian. Ashkenazi Jews often pick on their more secularized Sephardic counterparts, while official, "real" Indians like to show they can "out-Indian" the Wannabes. Let us look first at the latter phenomenon.

In an article in the *American Indian Quarterly* that appeared the same year as Malamud and Tabori's pieces, William Quinn distils his work experiences as an "ethnohistorian" at the Bureau of Indian Affairs into a sort of legal brief on the subject of Wannabe Indians. "The Southeast Syndrome: Notes on Indian Descendant

Recruitment Organizations" argues that Native American cultural associations in that region of the country are *not* Indian tribes; they do not deserve federal recognition and in fact do not even qualify as "authentic." In this position lurks a denial of Indian historicity that is similar to the disbelief many choose to harbor about the Jewish Holocaust. All Indians must "vanish" as though they had never existed. Quinn has a deep-seated antipathy toward any ethnicity that does not conform to the dominant, white, Anglo-Saxon, Protestant, male technocracy of contemporary America.

He defines the Southeast Syndrome in a very precise way. It is a resurgence of Indian identity or "pan-Indianism" among descendants "and others" in the former territories of the Five Civilized Tribes. The brief historical background he gives by way of a lead-in is not very sympathetic to Indians real or imagined. We encounter the same truisms found in most U.S. history textbooks. What is original on Quinn's part is the sleight of hand that comes next. The Indians who remain behind after the forced removals of the 1830s suddenly become *descendants of Indians*, not actual Indians per se. True Indians have been relegated to history, at least in the reservation-free (we are tempted to say *judenrein*) Southern states.

Not all the Indians of the southeastern tribes, however, went west. Small bands of Cherokee, Creek, and other tribes either hid in the hills, swamps, or similarly remote places or obtained official permission to remain. Others, mostly individuals of mixed blood, simply relocated to the next county or area where they were not known as

Indian and homesteaded or otherwise established themselves as white by repudiating, at least publicly, their Indian heritage.

Note that in the eyes of the government, these "individuals of mixed blood" cease to be Indians once they are severed from their tribe. Their children and grandchildren are merely "descendants," some of them only alleged and unproved descendants at that. These watered down versions of the Indians of history strive for a legitimate status they will never obtain. Since they do not live in Indian Country they cannot be Indian. Because they are modern and contemporary they cannot be granted any historicity. Ultimately, all Indians are illusions. If we rub our eyes they may disappear. The land will be free of any encumbrance.

There are disturbing subtexts of a racist nature here. Quinn hints that the mixed bloods were the result of miscegenation in the first place. Some white men will always want to "turn Injun" on you! Even though the mixed bloods were once bona fide members of Indian communities, at a time when Indian nations enjoyed autonomy and power, their descendants are to be repudiated.

To Quinn's horror, these "descendant organizations" actively recruit members, apply for federal and state recognition as Indian tribes (a process which if it is successful brings entitlements such as educational assistance) and promote what he judges to be a phony, unfounded culture, one based on books and media images.

What seems to worry Quinn most are the ridiculous lengths to which Wannabes will go to give themselves the appearance (*illusion*) of being Indian. The horrors of "reverse acculturation" are specifically mentioned.

About the best Quinn can make of such behavior is that the "descendants" suffer from a form of "selective perception." In other words, they are delusional. Having played lawyer, he now acts out the part of psychologist. These illegitimate groups are probably "harmless and may indeed serve as a method for the externalization of unconscious archetypes or suppressed elements within the psyche." But they still constitute a serious burden to "the solemn guardians of Indian rights and dedicated champions of Indian causes." We know who these guardians are, of course. One wonders only at what point, and why, they ceased to be Indian fighters and started being the sacred friend of the Indian.

Why is Quinn so hostile to Indian culture? Why does he approve only of "his" Native Americans? And how are "Indian recruitment organizations" different from Masonic lodges, Polish-American Leagues, the Sierra Club, churches, professional associations like the Guild of Graphic Artists, genealogical societies or even trade associations?

The answers touch on a type of racism we can observe in another group: the exclusivity many Jews show toward other Jews. As suggested by the Jewish writers glanced at in this chapter, there are two types of Jews, the "white" assimilated Jew, often unduly entranced by the materialism of the New World, and "other" Jew, more ethnic, pious, poor and suffering, but also mystical and noble.

Sometimes they appear in the same person, with a consequential seesawing between self-loathing and self-congratulation. These two ethnic breeds are replaced, or displaced, by good and bad Indians in the work of Efros and Silkiner. Tabori gives his Weisman character the choice of becoming a "white" Jew (the perpetrator) or the other "brown" kind (a victim). Weisman chooses to be a victim and he dies in passivity; his counterpart Rotgesicht takes action and rides off the victor. Weisman ends up being a good Jew and Rotgesicht, a bad Indian. A clue to Rotgesicht's true nature is his bland, good-ole-American disguise of "redface," artificially produced by a layer of Coppertone tanning cream.

The opposition between the two types of Jews is demonstrated by the Cold War that sometimes erupts on a social level between Ashkenazim and Sephardim. Subconsciously, and sometimes overtly, the former claim to be "more" Jewish than the latter. Underneath this antagonism is a denial of historicity to Spanish Crypto-Jews. The classic study is B. Netanyahu's *The Marranos of Spain*, in which the problem is supposedly resolved by an appeal to halakhic law.

With a sophistry worthy of the Office of Recognition, Netanyahu first takes care to distinguish the New Christians in post-1391 Spain from the Anusim ("Forced Ones") of an earlier era.

> "The forced convert is not an outright traitor, as the real convert was considered to be, but he is nevertheless a cowardly deserter; he should realize that he has

committed a disgraceful act and his bearing should be one of shame and humiliation; only a long process of repentance through sufferance could obliterate his shame and sin... What can be deduced... regarding the shifting attitudes among the conversos toward both Christianity and Judaism can be safely summarized as follows. The attachment to Judaism was weakening; the trend toward Christianity was intensified... The conversion of many, which was at first forced, ended as a voluntary one... the number of real renegades was alarmingly increasing."

"The theory that the Marrano camp as a whole is to be regarded a Jewish camp appears fictitious even when applied to that early period [fifteenth century]. Already then it was drifting away from the Jewish fold... "

"The Marranos ought to be treated realistically according to what they actually were – not *unwilling*, but *willing* converts, and consequently traitors to the Jewish religion and enemies of the Jewish people."

Netanyahu stacks the cards against Marranos using much the same strategy as the U.S. government does with Indians. It is easy to see that this is a distinction without a difference. In both cases, it is a denial of historicity.

Wannabe Indians are scorned by "real" Indians because they pick and choose what customs they will adopt, because they have "a distorted notion of the way in which Indians live and behave in the 1980s," according to Quinn. In Netanyahu, Crypto-Jews are likewise locked out of their native identities because their practice of Judaism is "limited to the performance of *certain* Jewish rites only." Descendants of the Five Civilized Tribes are not backward enough to be Indians; Sephardim are not religious enough to be Jews. Neither Marranos nor Wannabe Indians have met their suffering quota. They are not entitled to the "recognized tribe " standing of a reservation Indian in politically correct 21st century America or to the protected status of a Holocaust survivor or Zionist in an age where Jewishness has been coopted by what Salo Baron called the "lachrymose school" of Judaic history and is defined too narrowly as *anti*-anti-Semitism. In an end run on fake Indians and false Jews, their aspirations are dismissed as delusions, and their ideals, illusions. While this is only in dreary officialdom, where the arbiters of identity are governmental bodies, the mainstream media and academia often take much the same reductionist positions if we are to judge from such writers as Stuart Hall and Paul du Gay in *Questions of Cultural Identity* (1996) and Paul Brodwin ("Bioethics in Action," 2005).

Fortunately, the figures we have examined from Malamud's *The People* and Tabori's *Weisman und Rotgesicht* suggest that the realities of ethnic identity and cultural affiliation in life and literature are more complicated, subtle and surprising.

SUGGESTED READINGS

Lisa Alther, *Washed in the Blood* (Macon: Mercer University Press, 2011). Multi-generational novel of the peoples of Appalachia.

Stephen Birmingham, *The Grandees: The Story of America's Sephardic Elite* (Ithaca: Syracuse University Press, 1997). And for the Ashkenazis among us Birmingham also wrote *"Our Crowd": The Great Jewish Families of New York*.

W. J. Cash, *The Mind of the South* (New York: Vintage, 1991). "No one, among the multitudes who have written about the South, has been more penetrating or more persuasive than Mr. Cash." — *The New York Times*

Miguel de Cervantes, *Don Quixote*, trans. Edith Grossman (New York: HarperCollins, 2003). The best translation of this masterpiece of world literature from Spain's Golden Age.

David M. Gitlitz and Linda Kay Davidson, *A Drizzle of Honey. The Lives and Recipes of Spain's Secret Jews* (New York: St. Martin's Griffin, 1999). Read the poetry and cook the dishes of your ancestors!

Elizabeth C. Hirschman, *Melungeons: The Last Lost Tribe in America* (Macon: Mercer University Press, 2005). Supplements Kennedy with important additions about culture and identity.

Elizabeth Caldwell Hirschman and Donald N. Yates, *The Early Jews and Muslims of England and Wales: A Genetic and Genealogical History* (Jefferson: McFarland, 2013); *Jews and Muslims in British Colonial America. A Genealogical History* (Jefferson: McFarland, 2012); *When Scotland Was Jewish.DNA Evidence, Archeology, Analysis of Migrations, and Public and Family Records Show Twelfth Century Semitic Roots.* Jefferson: McFarland, 2007). Trilogy on the background of Melungeons in Europe.

N. Brent Kennedy with Robyn Vaughan Kennedy, *The Melungeons. Resurrection of a Proud People. An Untold Story of Ethnic Cleansing in America.* Second, revised and corrected edition (Macon: Mercer University Press, 1997). "The book is a beginning to understanding a part of our historical origins which has been bypassed by those writing the history of the Appalachian region." —*West Virginia History*

Judith Martin, *Miss Manners' Guide to Excruciatingly Correct Behavior* (New York: W. W. Norton, 2005). See p. 246, "The Internet."

Nell Irwin Painter, *The History of White People* (W.W. Norton: New York, 2011). Survey of white supremacy theory in mainstream literature and science, from antiquity to the present day.

John Andrew Rice, *I Came out of the Eighteenth Century* (New York: Harper, 1942). Wonderful, curmudgeonly recollections of the Old South.

Cecil Roth , *The Spanish Inquisition* (New York: W.W. Norton, 1937). Classic study of Spain's persecution of Jews, 1390-1800.

Shlomo Sand, *The Invention of the Jewish People* (London: Verso, 2009). "Countering official Zionist historiography, Sand questions whether the Jewish People ever existed as a national group with a common origin in the Land of Israel/Palestine. He concludes that the Jews should be seen as a religious community comprising a mishmash of individuals and groups that had converted to the ancient monotheistic religion but do not have any historical right to establish an independent Jewish state in the Holy Land." —Leon T. Hadar, *Middle East Policy.*

Donald N. Yates, *Old Souls in a New World. The Secret History of the Cherokee Indians* (Phoenix: Panther's Lodge, 2013); *Cherokee Clans: An Informal History* (Phoenix: Panther's Lodge, 2011). Also available as audiobooks narrated by Rich Crankshaw. *Old World Roots of the Cherokee. How DNA, Ancient Alphabets and Religion Explain the Origins of America's Largest Indian Nation*, foreword by Richard Mack Bettis (Jefferson: McFarland, 2012). Audiobook narrated by Jack Chekijian.

ANCESTORS AND ENEMIES

ABOUT THE AUTHORS

Phyllis E. Starnes is a Melungeon descendant who lives in Harriman, Tennessee. For generations, her family has belonged to the original Stony Creek Primitive Baptist Church (now Pine Grove). She is Assistant Principal Investigator at DNA Consultants, where she administers the Melungeon DNA Project.

Donald N. Yates is a native of Cedartown, Georgia. He earned a Ph.D. in classical studies with a concentration on medieval Latin from the University of North Carolina at Chapel Hill. His latest book of history is *Old Souls in a New World: The Secret History of the Cherokee Indians*.

23475573R00142

Made in the USA
Charleston, SC
24 October 2013